INTRODUCTION TO WORLD RELIGIONS

DANTES/DSST* Study Guide

All rights reserved. This Study Guide, Book and Flashcards are protected under the US Copyright Law. No part of this book or study guide or flashcards may be reproduced, distributed or stored in a retrieval system, or transmitted in any form or by any means, electronic, mechanical, photocopying, recording, or otherwise, without the prior written permission of the publisher Breely Crush Publishing, LLC.

© 2012 Breely Crush Publishing, LLC

*DSST is a registered trademark of The Thomson Corporation and its affiliated companies, and does not endorse this book.

971122911143

Copyright ©2003 - 2012, Breely Crush Publishing, LLC.

All rights reserved.

This Study Guide, Book and Flashcards are protected under the US Copyright Law. No part of this publication may be reproduced, distributed or stored in a retrieval system, or transmitted in any form or by any means, electronic, mechanical, photocopying, recording, or otherwise, without the prior written permission of the publisher Breely Crush Publishing, LLC.

Published by Breely Crush Publishing, LLC
10808 River Front Parkway
South Jordan, UT 84095
www.breelycrushpublishing.com

ISBN-10: 1-61433-054-9
ISBN-13: 978-1-61433-054-7

Printed and bound in the United States of America.

*DSST is a registered trademark of The Thomson Corporation and its affiliated companies, and does not endorse this book.

Table of Contents

Chapter 1: An Overview of Religion

What is religion? That is a loaded question for most experts. Everyone tends to have a varied view of religion and how to define it. Wikipedia defines religion as "commonly understood as a group of beliefs or attitudes concerning an object (real or imagined), person (real or imagined), or system of thought considered to be supernatural, sacred, or divine, and the moral codes, practices, valued institutions, and rituals associated with such belief or system of thought." Sometimes people use the word "religion" as a way to describe faith or organized religion. However, most experts agree that religion is not a term easily defined.

General Characteristics of Religion

There are several general characteristics of religion, though they are not always necessary for a belief system to be considered a religion. There is the idea that something is holy or sacred, and then there is the response to it. Sometimes the response takes on the form of customs or rituals, and at other times it just involves an attitude.

The idea of holiness and the response to that idea is where belief systems come into play. There is a respect for both the rituals and the doctrine. The beliefs allow people to understand the holiness and the response as it relates to themselves and the world around them. While some traditions start off based on myth, theology or ritual, law quickly comes in to supplant those myths.

Rituals are a common aspect of religion, and they can be personalized rituals or community-based rituals. They involve things like rites of passage, sacrifice, sacrament, invocations, and more.

Besides rituals, there are also ethical codes that are often attached to religious beliefs. These codes tend to guide a society into knowing what is right and wrong, and they come with the weight and prestige of what the society considers holy.

Finally, there is a social aspect to most religions that make the community and integral part of the belief system. There are some solitary religions, but in most cases they are community-based. In some cases, religion cannot be considered without the community, with the leader of the society being the religious leader.

© 2012 Breely Crush Publishing, LLC

Although the term "religion" covers a range of beliefs and moral codes, there are varied ways that religion is studied and talked about. Basically, there are three approaches to religion, though the models are not mutually exclusive. There is the model that sees religions as social constructions and another model that sees religions as aspiring for a higher, more objective, truth. Finally, there is an approach that sees religion as an absolute truth. Often they are combined to give people a thorough overview of a certain religion.

Religion as a Description of Society

Anthropologists and sociologists tend to take the social construction of religions into the most consideration. Anthropologists study human behavior, and the science focuses on religion as a pattern of human behavior. They tend to look at religion from the outside, taking a neutral, scholarly approach and do not make a judgment as to whether or not the religion is true. These scientists tend to use religion as a way of explaining human behavior and experiences in different cultures.

Yet even the study of religion as a social construction has changed over time. Prior to the 20th Century, anthropologists asked themselves the question as to how religions started. Before that time, it was commonly believed that religion would cease to exist once science replaced it in the way humans thought. Much of the perspective was due to the work of Charles Darwin in that it focused on how evolution influenced belief systems.

Then the focus changed at the turn of the 20th century toward looking at the function of religion within a society. Bronislaw Malinowski (1884 – 1942) was convinced that culture had scientific laws that could be applied just as easily to religion. Things like food, sex, shelter, security, and more were all needs that a society used economies, politics, kinship, and religions to fill.

Then in the 1950's, scientists focusing on social construction began looking at religion more as a direct result of a society's values, ideas, and beliefs. Now religion was looked at as a relationship between beliefs. Scientists wanted to know the pattern of a religion.

While anthropologists were evolving in their approach to religion as a social construction, there was also the influence of psychologists and sociologists involved. Sigmund Freud was a great influence in that he theorized that the human mind, grounded in the libido, believed in a God-figure that came from the child's relationship with the father. Freud's theory was expanded into the concept of "projection," which is the idea that statements about religion are really statements about humanity. Social constructionists who adhered to this philosophy thought the only way they could understand religion was to interpret religion in human terms. While Freud denounced religion, other psychologists like William James (1842 – 1910) saw religion as a valuable way for people to live a positive life, helping people to accept the life condition.

Yet, by the early 20th century, sociologists like Emile Durkheim (1858 – 1917) asserted that religion was the way humans spoke about their social reality; they just put it into words about Gods rather than humanity. He thought it was necessary to hold the society together as a moral community, and he felt strongly that there was some reality in religion itself that held it together.

Religion from a Historical Point of View

For some scientists, the only way to objectively study religion is to take on a historical point of view. These historians focus on religion as it applies to certain events throughout history. Often these experts deal with certain texts or documentation that specifically pertains to religious doctrine, rituals, devotions, and more. They use these documents to construct the religious beliefs of the community.

The historical approach takes a look at religious trends over time and the impact of religion on events and vice versa. It takes a very external approach to religion, examining the beliefs and rituals in an objective and scientific way. Often this approach is combined with a sociological or theological view of religion.

Religion from a Theological Viewpoint

The third approach to religion is to examine beliefs from a theological point of view. This approach is much more introspective, looking at the religion from the inside. Often people within the religion itself take this approach. The theologians take a close look at the meaning of the doctrines and rituals.

While other approaches take on a more objective view of religion, not passing judgment on the beliefs themselves, a theologian questions the validity of the belief system. They want to know if the beliefs are true or false and why people respond to those beliefs. The study from this point of view is always grounded in religious tradition.

Taking a theological viewpoint means taking a close look at the ethics and acts of worship of a religion. Often a theologian will investigate the religion with the idea that a

© 2012 Breely Crush Publishing, LLC

belief is true, and then the scientist explores the beliefs more fully. He or she will then relate the faith to the world around him or her and apply it to world situations.

Theologists tend to look at religion from a variety of angles. They may look at it from a critically analytical point of view or a historical point of view. There is also the systematic point of view in the attributes of the religion. Finally, there is the practical point of view that tends to look at the practical application of religion. Often, though, these approaches are combined to give theologians a deeper understanding of the religion.

Chapter 2: Primal Religions

Primal religions may be relegated by those in "developed" countries as nonsense, but in truth many tribes are significantly more religious that those in other societies. They live closer to the land, where they are at the mercy of nature and death, so they tend to feel that they are surrounded by evil. They have a strong understanding that they are surrounded by an invisible power, and each society has constructed a religious system that explains and connects them to this power.

This link means that primal religions have a way of meeting the needs of the people. In primal religions, the people tend to have a sense of human nature, and understanding of the fragility of life, and a dependence on the spirit world. The term "primal" is meant to show that these religions came before the "universal religions" like Christianity or Hinduism. These religions have been subject to demeaning terms like "heathen," "animistic," "savage," or "primitive," and those terms tend to be offensive to those that practice it.

Primal religions tend to have some common characteristics. There is often a strong belief in a spirit world where there are powers greater than those of man. Most of these religions contain a belief that we are not alone. This spirit power tends to be in everything and everyone, though in some religions it can be concentrated in one person. In other primal religions, the spirit powers are contained in Gods, although there are several primal religions that are monotheistic. Monotheistic means that they only believe in one God.

Another common characteristic in primal religions is the belief in the living dead. They believe that the dead communicate with the living, and that the ancestral spirits must be honored. Often this is considered "ancestor worship."

While ancestor worship is common, so is the dependence on myths. Most primal religions are based upon myths, or complicated stories that exhibit a religion's theology and philosophy. They also rely on dreams and visions to guide a person or community.

 © 2012 Breely Crush Publishing, LLC

Rituals are an important characteristic of primal religions. For many, the New Year involves some of the most important rituals. These rituals often combine the myth and an act of worship. Sometimes they culminate in a great festival or sacrifice.

Finally, most of these primal religions need a central figure to help with the activities and rituals. They are often referred to as a "medicine man." The medicine men tend to fill a number of roles like priest, healer, diviner, shaman, or medium. However, they are not magician or sorcerers as some outsiders have believed in the past.

Native North American Traditions

One of the areas that are seeing resurgence in primal beliefs is in the Native North American culture. For a while, the influence of Western Civilization had discredited and shunned the beliefs of these native peoples. However, with the recent lack of consideration for the environment, community, and spirituality, many of these cultures are turning back to their religious roots.

The native people of North America have a wisdom rooted in the past. They have a strong emphasis placed on the teaching of the ancients. They may have a One Great Spirit. For the Inuit people of Southeast Alaska, the closest thing they have to One Great Spirit is the Old Woman who lived under the sea.

The Inuit people practiced Shamanism with an underlying animist principle. This principle is also common in North American tribes, as it asserts that everything has a form of spirit, which can be influenced by supernatural entities. They acknowledged the fragility of humanity, like many other Native North American cultures. They believed that their existence was based entirely on the consumption of souls, animal souls that were thought to be equal to humans, and so they gave great respect to the animals they hunted.

The Lakota is another North American culture that practices shamanism, but they do have One Great Spirit called Wakan Tanka. They place a lot of emphasis on visions and dreams. They have a number of rituals that honor the spirits in the things that surround them. They often perform rites of passage that encourage visions, and it is said that a Lakota boy cannot become a man until he has a vision. They have a strong idea of good and bad in the world, and they do recognize that there is a salvation.

While the Lakota have their Great Spirit, and the Inuit their animist principles, the Hopi worship Kokopelli, the humpbacked flutist that took part in weddings and gave fetuses to pregnant women. The Hopi also have a strong belief in salvation and the afterlife. They believe that good people go west and become kachinas.

 # Native West African Traditions

There are several cultures in West Africa that also practice primal religions. These religions tend to be handed down through generations, and the elders are respected as the ultimate authority. Most often West African religions focus on humanity itself versus natural or supernatural phenomena. The religions emphasize human values as they pertain to the most important thing – community. They have elaborate initiation and marriage rites and do not believe that life ends in death. They believe people go on to the realm of the dead, and the good people who are dead continue to communicate with their living descendents.

One example of a West African culture that is slowly losing touch with their religion is the Dogon. Today many of the Dogon people no longer practice the old religion due to the influx of Islam and Christianity, but it does not mean that the old practices are lost. The people continue to conduct rituals, while mostly for show, that have been passed down over generations. They have a strong belief that there is danger all around us, and there is a fight going on between good and evil. They believe that there is a world of the dead.

Another West African culture that contains aspects of primal religions is the Yaruba tribe. Many people consider their religion to be the roots of Voodoo. They have a belief in one Supreme Being known as the Grand Maitre. There are also some lesser Gods known as Ioa. They have significant rituals to honor the Gods, and the sacred drums are always played in groups of three. In their rituals, the Yaruba enter a trance-like state for hours that prompted the idea of zombies.

 # Zoroastrianism

There isn't much definitive information about Zoroastrianism, but it is believed to have been developed around 1000 BC, by Zoroaster. Zoroaster claimed to have seen God, Ahura Mazda, in a vision at the age of thirty. The main teachings are that there is one supreme deity, which is Ahura Mazda, or Wise Lord. Also, there are Modes of Good Action, such as good thought or sense. There are Modes of Evil which oppose Ahura Mazda. Zoroaster saw the soul as a scene of struggle between good and bad forces. He also believed in the final victory of Ahura Mazda, and the judgment of individual souls.

 © 2012 Breely Crush Publishing, LLC

CHAPTER 3: Hinduism

Hinduism is one of the oldest religions in the world, as it has been in development for over 5,000 years. It consists of various schools of thought, but it has been said that Hinduism is more of a culture than a religion. It has no set creed, no institutional culture, no founder, and no prophet. They believe that everyone is Hindu, because they are born a Hindu, though not all Hindu born people practice the religion. The practices of Hinduism are so varied that one scientist asserted that the only universal aspect of Hinduism is the Indian character and the reverence of the cow.

Despite the confusion over the variance in practice, Hinduism does have some common themes. They believe in Dharma, which is the idea of an individual's ethics, duties and obligation. Samsara, or reincarnation, and karma, or the cause-effect relationship of actions, both find their way into the beliefs of most Hindus. Samsara is governed by karma, and continues until one achieves Moksha, or salvation. Therefore most Hindus believe that they cannot achieve this higher consciousness or Supreme Devine, unless their actions are virtuous.

History of Hinduism

The Hindu does not believe that historical events pose much relevance to the religion itself. The Sanatana Dharma is made up of principles that have no beginning and will have no end. Experts believe in two schools of thought regarding the origin on Hinduism. Some believe that the religion was founded between 1500 and 1300 BC. Others believe that Hinduism was formed in 3102 BC.

Those who believe the religion was founded between 1500 and 1300 BC base their information on the Rig Veda. Those who give the foundation of Hinduism and earlier date take their stance from examining the Mahabharata, which noted the star positions at the birth of Sri Krishna. However, secular historians do not necessarily agree with those dates.

Early Hinduism was made up mostly of the Vedic religion along with the religions of the Dravidian and Indus Valley people. During this time, it is believed that the early Hindus lived in a matriarchal society, exemplified by a mother-God portrayed as the giver of life. However, the mother-God was not alone, in that there has been archeological evidence showing a male God known as Trimurti. He had horns and three faces, later to be described as Brahma, Vishnu, and Shiva. He is also described as the "Lord of Beasts." During this time, Hinduism was often referred to as "Vedism."

By the middle of the second millennium BC, the Aryan people invaded, and they brought with them their language and religious traditions. While the Aryans did not make Hindus give up the old religion, it did assert an influence of being "world-affirming." It enhanced the already established yoga, renunciation, and purification rites by creating openness with nature. It was during this period that a lot of the Rig Veda, or "songs of knowledge," were written. While the songs are addressed to one God, several Gods are featured within the songs.

In the Rig Veda, there is a distinction between the purusha, or World Soul, and the prakriti, or substance. It states that there can be no life without sacrifice, and there are several divisions of the World Soul that is the social order. The Brahimi, or priestly order, is the mouth of the World Soul and the rulers, or Rajanya, are the arms. Landowners, merchants, and bankers (vaishya) become the thighs while workers, artisans, and serfs (shudra) are the feet. However, despite the World Soul was seemingly divided equally, but the Brahimi were quickly gaining more power than others.

By 600 BC, the priestly order above all others was an accepted practice. However, new movements known as Jainism and Buddhism challenged the rising priestly order. Also, a new movement by people known as Upanishads redirected the Vedantic traditions. In fact, the Upanishads had more influence over what we know as Hinduism that Jainism or Buddhism, which Hindu teachers thought unorthodox beliefs. The Upanishads are a group of treatises which are indispensable in studying religions of India. They are the philosophical texts (scriptures) of Hindu. The most commonly taught veda, and most important veda, is the Rig Veda. It contains over 1,000 hymns which reflect the devotion to family during the Vedic age. The Bhagavad Gita is sometimes referred to as the Manual of Mankind. It is 700 verses long, and describes a conversation between Arjuna and Lord Krishna, who reveals himself to be the Supreme Being.

The Upanishads were not as concerned with Gods or ritual sacrifice. Instead, they focused on the Brahman, or reality. They wanted to explore human consciousness, and felt that the most basic parts of the human self were really the reality that supported the cosmos. Like Buddhists and the Jain, the Upanishads wanted to overcome the anxiety and frustration of human existence. They wanted to find the essence of permanence within the individual, despite the knowledge that life had flux and impermanence.

From 300 BC to 300 AD, we see the emergence of Classical Hinduism. Buddhism and Jainism were experiencing widespread growth, and Vedantic orthodoxy was also developing. It was the time that bhakti, or devotion to one God, was entering the religion. The Aryan influence was coming together with the traditions, and the religion either replaced the Vedantic deities with older Gods or found older Gods to identify with the deities.

© 2012 Breely Crush Publishing, LLC

It was also during this time that the old Hindu stories were written, as they had previously been circulating as legend. The stories are epics that describe the fight between good and evil in humanity and our affairs. In the end, these epics assured Hindus that order will prevail and offered them the knowledge that there is always a way out of chaos. The Ramayama and Mahabharata divide history into cycles. They are stories that exemplify the need for purpose and meaning, even when the world is in disorder. In the Mahabharata, there is a section called "Bhagavad-Gita," or Song of the Lord, that has even been referred to as the "bible of the Hindu." It explains that salvation is something anyone can attain.

The most widely distributed stories, though, are those of the Krishna cycle. In the Bhagavata Purana, the tale begins with stories of his miraculous birth and infancy. It goes on to tell of how he lived among the cowherds of Vrindaban and his powers of seduction, which have prompted believers to see him not only as a father, friend, and elder figure, but also a lover and husband. The stories are meant as lessons to the believer to be an example they will want to emulate. It is from the story of Krishna, who is often shown as a cowherd, which the worship of the cow came about. It is said that even feeding the cow is a form of worship. Some Hindus even take it so far as to be vegetarians, though most Hindus do eat meat.

With the uprising of the Upanishads came the end of the Vedantic tradition, and the focus on individual identity and the One Reality, or monism, came into being. While it is the primary focus of modern Hinduism, it has been interpreted in a number of ways. The sutras were created, though they were often too brief for people to get a good understanding of the religion. Then commentaries were written to explain Hindu thought. Shankara (788-820 AD), Ramanuja (d. 1137 AD), and Madhva (1197-1276 AD) were three of the foremost interpreters of the Vedanta.

Hindu Philosophy

Traditionally there are six darshanas, or systems, in the Hindu religion. They are called the Samkhya, Yoga, Nyaya, Vaisheshika, Purva Mimamsa, and Vedanta.

Samkhya

The first is called Samkhya, and it is the oldest of the darshanas. Samkhya asserts that there are two eternal realities called the purusha and prakrti, or souls and nature or matter. There are many parushas, but they have no qualities. They only watch the prakrti. When the equilibrium between the two is upset, the world order must be restored. While other forms of dualism state that there is a difference in the mind and the body, Samkhya states that the difference is in the self and matter.

Yoga

While Samkhya started off by being atheistic, it spawned Yoga, which has a theistic aspect. The primary text of Yoga is the Bhagavad-Gita, divided into four systems. Yoga is described in the Bhagavad-Gita as a way anyone can join in union with The Supreme, although there is some disagreement on the nature of The Supreme. Yoga contains the concept of a personal God, or Ishvara, upon which it is ideal to meditate. It has adopted aspects of Vedantic monism and the Upanishads. It encourages people to gain control over the personal self by gaining awareness over feelings, thoughts, and actions. Karma yoga is based off of Bhagavad Gita. It is the "discipline of action" and is used in achieving perfection through action. Bhakti yoga is the idea of forming loving relationships, which help form relationships with God.

Nyaya

Nyaya is another school of Hindu thought, and it is based upon the Nyaya Sutras. It is a system of logic similar to that seen in Western science and philosophy. It is often compared to Aristotelian logic. Nyaya sees the acquiring of knowledge could release a person from his or her suffering. There are four sources of knowledge: perception, inference, comparison, and testimony, and these four sources can be valid or invalid. As the Nyaya philosophy developed so did logical proofs for the existence of Ishvara, or God, which they used during their arguments with the Buddhists.

Vaisheshika

The fourth school of Hindu thought is Vaisheshika, which was founded by Kanada. It asserts an atomic pluralism in that everything in the universe can be reduced to a specific number of atoms. God is thought to be the essential force that creates a consciousness in those atoms. Originally Vaisheshika was created independently from the Nyaya, because it differed in one critical way: the Vaisheshika believed that there were only two sources for valid knowledge, not four. They believed that only perception and inference could provide valid knowledge. However, their closely related beliefs led to their eventual merger.

Purva Mimamsa

The Purva Mimamsa school of Hindu thought asserts that a person has to have an unquestionable faith in the Vedas. They must have regular performances of the yajnas, or fire sacrifices. They believe that the yajnas and mantras have a power that is the sustenance of all activity in the universe. Therefore, to the Purva Mimamsa places a strong emphasis on dharma. However, with the Purva Mimamsa, there is not an exclusion of the need for "release" as an ultimate aim, as exhibited by the other Hindu schools of thought. Instead, the early Purva Mimamsa believed that there needed to be a right action, which was not a selfish desire to be free, but a salvation though the prescriptions of the Vedas. However, this viewpoint changed later as they began to teach God and mukti related doctrines. There is now a focus on jnana, or enlightened activity that al-

 © *2012 Breely Crush Publishing, LLC*

lows the soul to escape from its constraints. Purva Mimamsa now influences all Hindu ritual, ceremony, and religious law.

Vedanta

Sometimes Vedanta is referred to as the Uttara Mimamsa school of thought, because they focus more on the Upanishads teachings rather than the rituals of the Brahmanas. The Vedanta believe that the Jivatma, or consciousness of the self, is not distinguishable from the consciousness of the Supreme Spirit, or Brahman. There are six sub-schools of Vedanta, because the aphorisms of the Vedanta sutras are rather cryptic.

 # Social Dharma

There are two main concepts in classical Hinduism – Karma and Dharma. Karma is often referred to as a person's actions, which can be defined a good or bad. These actions would influence a person's destiny. Therefore, dharma came to play as religious duty and a social order required by religious law. Responsible action was definable by one's class, so social dharma was created, and even the Bhagavad-Gita deems it wrong to try and fulfill someone else's dharma. In Hinduism, ethical pursuits were all relative except for that which released the person from the cycle of rebirth. Many of the rules of dharma are outlined in the Laws of Manu.

There are four separate orders in Hinduism's social dharma. There is the student, householder, hermit, and ascetic. Each order has a specific dharma. In Hinduism the ritual acts of an order and ethics are combined. Today, Hindus place more emphasis on progress than time cycles. They tend to have more a focus on things like being truthful, kind, and loving while still retaining the goal of the common good.

 # Hindu Rituals

There are several Hindu rituals that are performed as acts of worship. Back when the Aryans invaded, most of the rituals were held outside around a sacred fire. It was not until the Hindus moved to the Indus Valley that they began to build temples for worship. In order to enter a Hindu temple, a worshipper has to prepare oneself with purification rites. For example, a Vaishnavite wishing to worship in the morning would have to perform sixteen tasks, like washing the feet and rinsing the mouth. Even while purification rights were being performed, bells are rung, incense is burned, and ritual music plays.

After purification, the worshipper pays respects to the God and then makes requests. After the respects are made, water and prasada are presented as a divine banquet. The prasada is the first offering of food before it is given out to the worshippers. There is also a statue present in the temple that is the symbol of the divine presence.

A more sophisticated worshipper would have a temple in which each part carried a symbolic meaning. For instance, the central part of the temple would represent the heart of the worshipper and the tower would represent the flight of the spirit toward heaven.

Finally, priests would read the Vedas to the worshippers, and then anyone from the first three classes could read the mantras. Then the worshippers go around the temple making gifts of flowers or money, always keeping it to their right shoulder.

The rituals of temple worship are very individualistic rather than congregational, which is why the rituals of worship in the home are just as important. However, the home-based rituals are largely based upon class, with the priestly class having the most detailed rituals to perform. Twice born Hindus have rites that they must perform three times per day. The type of sacred thread they wear during worship is based upon class, for example the vaishya use wool. Also, each caste has a specific mark on the forehead and on other parts of the body.

Besides daily prayer rituals, Hindus also have a number of festivals that, for the most part, are used to mark seasonal changes or the activities of Ramayana and Krishna. Of all the festivals, the most popular is Holi, which a festival associated with Krishna and held in the Spring. This is one of the few times that caste is disregarded. Its primary focus is pleasure.

Another well-known festival is Divali, which is held in autumn and associated with Kali and Lakshmi. Pilgrims travel to centers such as Vrindaban, Varanasi, and Alla-habad. Hundred of thousands of individuals make the pilgrimage to one of these areas. It is a festival of lights and presents. It is said that Lakshmi visits each home that is lit by a lamp.

Hindu Symbols

There are several symbols in Hinduism that have a variety of meanings. There is one symbol commonly worn on the body, and three that are revered symbols in not only the religion, but the culture, too.

Tilaka

The tilaka is a symbol that is most commonly place on the forehead between the eye-brows. It can sometimes be placed on other parts of the body. The symbol signifies the

Hindus need to grow toward supramental consciousness, also known as opening the third eye. In all Hindus it is a mark of faith, but in married women, it also means that they are married or auspicious. Modern Hindu women tend to wear it as decoration, or Bindi, on the forehead.

Aum/Om

The Aum is the sacred symbol of Hinduism as it represents the Supreme Being in its three aspects – Brahma, Vishnu, and Shiva. It is also referred to as "Om." The Aum is the symbol of the Hindu Dharma, and it represents all existence and all of nature into the one Reality. Most often Hindus wear the symbol on necklaces. Upanishads it is an affirmation.

Swastika

The Swastika is considered by Hindus to be a noble symbol. It symbolizes both the action of the Principle on Manifestation and the purity of the soul. It is often rotated in four directions to represent the Vedas and a harmonious whole. Despite the corruption of the symbol by the Nazis, it is still a widespread symbol in the Indian subcontinent.

Mandala

Finally, the Mandala is based on the importance of the number six in Hinduism. It symbolizes Analogy. Sometimes it comes in an interpretation that intertwines two triangles, one being fire and the other is water. It is used to symbolize the perfect union of the masculine and feminine principles.

Hindu Worship

As can be seen by the Hindu rituals, Hindu worship is a very individualized act. The worship is performed with the ultimate goal being moksha, or deliverance. It is karma-marga, or path to deliverance, that dictates a person's dharma. Action, to a Hindu, is a command.

The act of worship comes by way of devotion or love. Through the temple rites and daily worship, a Hindu shows a commitment to God. There is a belief in the idea of a human response to divine grace. It is only through bhakti that one can achieve salvation, and it is the bhakti that demands Hindu worship. The Hindu does not necessarily worship the idol, but instead the idol is a focus through which the God is worshipped, as God cannot take on any real form.

© 2012 Breely Crush Publishing, LLC

CHAPTER 4: Buddhism

Buddhism is a religion based upon the teaching of Buddha, who is said to have spent years in spiritual cultivation to discover the true nature of reality, or enlightenment. Buddhism was mainly concentrated in the Indian sub-continent, but has now increased to worldwide popularity. It is considered a major world religion and has over 350 million followers.

In Buddhism, any person can become enlightened through the study of Buddha's teachings and their practical application. Buddhists are expected to live a life of virtue and morality, and they are to purify their minds. They seek a state of nirvana, or moksha, through the eightfold path and middle way.

The Life of Buddha

Historical evidence has proven that Buddha actually existed. He was born in approximately 560 BC in Shuddhodanna, a rajah of a small principality around Lumbini. His birth name was Siddharta, which meant "one who has reached his goal." Buddha is normally referred to as Gautama, which is the name of a prominent Hindu teacher from which Siddharta was descended. Therefore, Buddha is known as Siddharta Gautama.

After a prediction that the prince would either become a great ruler or a homeless wanderer, his father sheltered him from all outside influences. He received an education in the arts and sciences, and he admitted that he was rather spoiled. By 16 he was married to Gopa and had a harem. He had one son, who he named Rahula, which means chain. Buddha stated that it was during this time he felt he was in chains.

By 29, Buddha decided to leave his life of privilege behind. He felt no satisfaction with his current life of wealth, so now he would be homeless. Before he was to leave his home for the last time, he went on three journeys in which he was faced with the suffering of the world. He was told that it was the fate of humanity to suffer, and this was troublesome to Buddha.

Buddha left on a fourth journey in which he discovered that life's pleasures are just vanity and worthless. He had met a cheerful monk on this trip that was perfectly content and joyful having only a begging bowl. The revelation opened up a longing in Buddha for real knowledge.

    © *2012 Breely Crush Publishing, LLC*

After traditional Hindu methods failed to give Buddha true knowledge, he came to Uruvela and lived for a time in extreme self-denial with five other followers. He managed only to harm his own health, and realized that this was not the way to true knowledge. Despite his companion's disgust at his renouncing of this life of self-denial, he chose to return to how he came to his first revelation. He sat under a fig tree.

It was under this fig tree that Buddha became the Buddha and reached the highest point of his knowledge. He saw that enlightenment came in three stages. The first night he saw his past lives passing by. The second night he had a supernatural vision of the cycle of birth, death, and rebirth. By the third night, he was revealed the four holy truths.

Since Buddha was now "the enlightened one," he could have entered nirvana immediately, and was tempted by the demon Mara to enter that state. However, Buddha resisted the temptation in order to teach the common people how to reach enlightenment, even though he was not sure that they were ready for the knowledge. His first sermon was at Benares, where his five former companions became his first disciples.

Buddha discarded the caste system, and the only people he excluded from his order were women. The caste system is very strict, where people are defined in different social standing based on their job or family ties. People from other castes cannot marry each other or even touch those of a different class. In the beginning, he believed women were responsible for keeping the cycle of birth in motion making them dangerous. His stepmother and cousin finally convinced him to allow women in the order, and he reluctantly allowed it. He predicted that his teachings would have lasted 1,000 years, but with women it would only last 500. History has proved him wrong.

Still, Buddha continued to travel around northeastern India teaching and living as a beggar-monk. By the age of 80, Buddha became ill and died in the village of Kushinagara. Legend says that there was a great earthquake when his body was burned.

 # *Early Buddhism*

As Buddhism grew, disputes arose on minor points. A second council was held to resolve the issues, but ended up creating a schism between the elders, or Sthaviras, and the majority, the Mahasanghikas. The elders stated that the majority was trying to dilute the religion by ignoring certain rules. Yet the majority believed that the elders were trying to introduce new rules that were never sanctioned by Buddha.

Buddhism spread across India, yet as it came in contact with other religions; it became necessary for Buddhists to formalize the teachings of Buddha. The formalized teachings highlighted the differences in the Buddhist sects. Buddhist supas, or memorials, were built throughout India, thanks mostly to the efforts of Maurya's King Asoka. Buddhism began to spread into Afghanistan and Central Asia, as well as Sri Lanka and China.

Emperor Asoka inherited the throne of Magadha (which controlled India) in 273 BC. With it he inherited a fiercely resistant kingdom along the Bay of Bengal. He felt so bad about the suffering of the people he conquered that he publicly embraced Buddhism and began to help it spread. He even reduced and then abolished the meat consumption at the palace and then banned killing certain types of animals throughout the land. He said that he would practice gentleness and bear all wrongs done to him with as much meekness and patience as possible.

 # Divisions of Buddhism

As the early Buddhist religion began to split off, several sects developed. There is the Theravada, Mahayana, and Vajrayanna. The elders formed the Theravada, while the majority created the Mahayana. Vajrayanna did not emerge until later in the evolution of Buddhism.

 # Theravada

Theravada means "teaching of the ancients," and it is sometimes referred to as the "Southern Tradition." The Theravadins believe that they are keeping to Buddha's earliest teachings in which it is very difficult to become Buddha and a relentless effort is needed to be a holy man. They see nirvana as the absence of things, or negative ideas. They place a strong emphasis on the effort one places to reach salvation, believing that no divine assistance is available. They disapprove of rituals and images. They do not believe that people should pray to Buddha, as he has already been swallowed up in nirvana.

It is this strictness that makes Theravada very difficult for the masses. In some areas it has been modified to include the worship of spirits and demons, so that it can be practiced by ordinary people. In traditional Theravada, only a monk can achieve nirvana, which is why many people spend a portion of their lives in a monastery. They also do not believe that Siddharta Guatama is the only Buddha. In fact, they believe there were six Buddhas before Siddharta Guatama and they predict one to come, Maitreya.

          © 2012 Breely Crush Publishing, LLC

Mahayana

The Mahasanghikas, who disagreed with the Theravadins, believe that everyone can achieve salvation, not just a choice few, making it more humane and magnanimous. The development of Mahayana used the basic teaching of Theravada and then brought in teaching from other texts which modernized the things Buddha taught.

Mahayana doctrine differs from Theravada in that they believe there are as many Buddhas as grains of sand united in the absolute being known as "Dharmakaya." Identifying the Dharmakayaallows one to identify it with the original Buddha, Adibuddha. Adibuddha has been enlightened for eternity.

Mahayana Buddhism has a very concrete idea of nirvana as a paradise created at the request of Adibuddha for all who pray and worship him. The name of this paradise is Sukhavati, and upon entry the hindrances of life will be removed.

Vajrayana

While Theravada and Mahayana Buddhism were created early on in the religions, Vajrayana came later on. It is a version of Mahayana Buddhism that consists of mystical, occult, and magical elements that has some of its basis in Indian Tantrism. Vajrayana desires for followers to enter into emptiness so that they can identify with the absolute. Most often a follower will work with a guru and commit to a constant and devoted religious practice. They use mantras, which are considered magical sayings recited repeatedly, that are to go out to the furthest reaches of the universe.

Vajrayana Buddhism also encourages mudra, or the use of specific physical gestures. There are special movements that show the being's desire to be united with the divine. In Tibet this has taken on a sexual element in Shaktism, where an orgiastic worship allows the worshiper to join with the universal feminine, and thus realizes the unity of all things. However, Shaktism is not looked upon well by other, stricter movements of Buddhism.

Finally, the mandala, or meditation circle, is often used in Vajrayana. It is a circle shaped diagram that represents the relationship between the cosmos and sprits. When one contemplates on the mandala, it is said that he or she will gain an experience of the divine.

© 2012 Breely Crush Publishing, LLC

Modern Buddhism

For a while, Buddhism's popularity waned as Christianity became a rather popular movement throughout the region. However, today Buddhism and Islam are seeing resurgence. The World Fellowship of Buddhists was founded in 1950, and it led to some missionary successes. Plus the sixth Buddhist Council, held from 1954 to 1956, added to the missionary work being done.

Late in the 1940's, the Prime Minister of Burma, U Nu, had an idea about social Buddhism. He saw land ownership and unfair distribution of property as a hindrance to a leisurely life. Without being free from care, they could not reach a religious goal, so he created an anti-capitalism society that was a Buddhist-based Marxism. Despite his efforts, it was not necessarily deemed a success.

However, Western Buddhism continued to grow with the immigration of Chinese and Japanese peoples. In the beginning these people practiced Mahayana Buddhism, but today they are united in the Buddhist Church of America. The religion contains not only Mahayana influences, but also those of Christianity and American culture.

While there are many different forms of Buddhism, they can be grouped in the two main branches, Theravada and Mahayana. Mahayana is the newer of the two forms and the more popular. Its origins are in the 1st century in India. The Mahayana believe that there are bodhistattva's which seek to become perfect (or in other words, seek "Buddahood") and help all sentient beings.

There is a third type of Buddhism called Vajrayana, which is sometimes classified as its own branch, and sometimes as a subcategory of Mahayana because they are similar.

Major Themes of Buddhism

It is important to realize that Buddhism itself is not an organized religion, which is why it is not always necessary to look at the religion in its total numbers. There are several different philosophies of Buddhism, but there are some central concepts essential to the teachings of Buddha himself.

© 2012 Breely Crush Publishing, LLC

Karma

Like Hinduism, karma is an essential concept of Buddhism. There is a cause and effect relationship in a person's actions. It has an impact on the moral and physical dimension. Buddha claimed that a person was in bondage to karma because of their good or bad actions.

Buddhists believe that it is possible to be liberated from karma though the understanding of the human condition and obedience to the right conditions. It does not mean that karma will just go away, but they will be free from its grip.

Reincarnation

Karma is an essential element of reincarnation. Depending on a person's actions, he or she would reap the results in reincarnation, or rebirth. A person's actions, thoughts, or speech would all impact the circumstances of reincarnation.

The Four Noble Truths

Buddha was revealed four noble truths when he sat under the fig tree:

All is Suffering
The first truth states that human existence itself is painful. Everything we experience – birth, death, illness, worry, and more – is suffering.

The Source of Suffering
The source of all suffering is desire and ignorance. Suffering comes when values are misplaced. Buddha taught that nothing in this world is worthy of ultimate reverence.

Removal of Suffering
Buddha taught that people could be released from their suffering.

The Way to the Removal of Suffering
The fourth truth revealed to Buddha is that there was an eightfold path that would release people from their suffering.

The Eightfold Path

Basically, the Eightfold Path is concerned with morality, spiritual discipline, and insight. It is a middle way between severe self-mortification and extreme sensuality. It is the only way to achieve nirvana. Here are the eight signposts:

- Right Knowledge: This means that one understands the four noble truths.
- Right Attitude: A person will adopt an attitude of goodwill and peace. He or she will shun sensual desire, hate, and malice.
- Right Speech: One will not lie, cheat, or gossip. There will be no unnecessary chatter. Speech must be used for wisdom, truth, and reconciliation.
- Right Action: All behavior should be moral. There will be no murder, stealing, or adultery.
- Right Occupation: If a person works, his work cannot be harmful to others.
- Right Effort: A person must put forth effort to develop deeds, words, and thoughts that are noble rather than giving in to evil impulses.
- Right Mindfulness: Careful consideration must be given to fostering an awareness of good thoughts, speech, action, and emotions.
- Right Composure: A holy man must be free from anything that hinders his quest, which can only be achieved by deep concentration.

Nirvana

Nirvana is the goal of a Buddhist's life. It is not the annihilation of the self, which is a common misconception of Buddhism. Instead it is a transformation of human consciousness achieved through Dharma. It is best described by a piece of Buddhist scripture known as the Tripitaka:

"Nirvana is the area where there is no earth, water, fire, and air; it is not the region of infinite space, nor that of infinite consciousness; it is not the region of nothing at all, nor the border between distinguishing and not distinguishing; not this world nor the other world; where there is neither sun nor moon. I will not call it coming and going, nor standing still, nor fading away nor beginning. It is without foundation, without continuation and without stopping. It is the end of suffering."

© 2012 Breely Crush Publishing, LLC

Buddhist Symbols

The Eight Spoked Buddha Wheel

The eight-spoked Buddha wheel, or Dharmachakra, is the symbol of Buddha turning the wheel of truth or law. There are eight spokes that symbolize the Eight-fold Path. The symbols in the center of the wheel symbolize Buddha, Dharma, and Sangha (or spiritual community).

Bodhi Tree

The Bodhi Tree is a symbol of the fig tree that Buddha sat under when he achieved enlightenment. While trees were already worshiped in India, it was a natural progression to worship the Bodhi Tree and Leaf.

Lion

The lion is a potent Buddhist symbol of strength and power. Sometimes Buddha's teachings are referred to as a "lion's roar," because they contain such strength and power.

Three Precious Jewels

The Three Precious Jewels are meant to symbolize the three pillars of Buddhism – Buddha, Dharma, and Sangha.

The Eight Auspicious Symbols

These eight symbols are most popular in Tibet. They are the umbrella, for protection from harmful activities and the golden fish to represent good fortune and having no fear. The treasure vase represents the riches available in the Buddhist teachings, and the lotus is a symbol of a person's overall purification. The conch symbolizes the melodious teachings, and the endless knot shows that everything is interrelated. The dharma wheel is also one of these symbols. Finally, the victory banner symbolizes the victory over all the negatives of the world.

Buddhist Worship

Buddhists worship either in a home or in a temple. At home, they will usually have a room for worship that contains a statue of Buddha, candles, and incense. Temples are also varied, but often they are designed to incorporate the five elements of fire, air, earth, water, and wisdom. Stupas are stone structures built over Buddha's relics or his teachings.

Worshippers will usually sit on the floor, barefoot, and face an image of Buddha. They will begin chanting. They will also listen to monks chanting portions of religious texts. Sometimes instruments accompany the chanting.

CHAPTER 5: Confucianism

Confucianism is the philosophical system that came from the teachings of an early Chinese sage named Confucius. Confucianism has a profound impact on the moral, social, political, and religious thought. It is still debated whether Confucianism is a philosophical system or a "state religion" as it was during imperial China.

Early Chinese Traditions

Chinese religion is not one that grew out of other belief systems, but was developed in isolation. This isolation has made information about early Chinese religions rather scarce. During the Shang Dynasty (1766 – 1122 BC), there are few details about the role religion played in the life of the Shang. What is known is that the Shang lived in a world where their lives were strongly influenced by spirits and powers. They made sacrifices to appease the spirits so that they could achieve successes.

The Shang used a complex system of divination in order to understand the wishes of the spirits. The diviner would ask a question of the spirits, as the king commanded, and then place a record of the answer and question on the carapace of a turtle or the shoulder blade of an ox. They had a strong belief in the balance of nature, later seen in the concept of Yin and Yang. It also was influential in the continuing concern for the well being of all people.

The Chou (or Zhou in some spellings) dynasty began in 1122 BC and would not end until 325 BC. The Chou religion invoked the Mandate of Heaven in which divine right governed the ruler. Divine right means that God chose the ruling family or King because it was His wish that they rule. Divine right is usually passed from father to son through blood lines. There was also a strong belief in the worship of ancestors that Confucius would take further in his teachings. Still, there was also a continuing concern for the well being of humanity even throughout this dynasty, but with the Chou is was High Heaven itself that was concerned with the people.

Life and Teachings of Confucius

Confucius (551 – 479 BCE) was a social philosopher whose teachings had a profound impact on Easter Asia over the centuries. His teachings continue today, though they were not necessarily accepted during his lifetime.

There is not much written on Confucius' family. We know that he was born to an aristocratic family, but tradition asserts that he was orphaned. When he was younger, Confucius served in the government, but retired at age 35 in frustration. He had tried to present his political ideas to the Feudal Lords, but they would not listen. He was against tyranny and encouraged leaders to use clemency and civilize the people. It was at the age of 40 that he created an academy to teach Confucianism to the masses, as he was not discriminating on the basis of class. At some point we know that he was married and had a son and a daughter.

While Confucius showed no discrimination to class in his teachings, it did not mean he did not have his downfalls. He showed an outward contempt for businessmen and farmers. He also looked down upon women. He believed that a wife should be completely devoted to her husband, a son to his father, and ministers to their masters in order to maintain an orderly government.

Most of what we know about Confucius's teaching comes from recollections of his disciples. Plus, in the Qin Dynasty, there was the Burning of the Books and Burying of the Scholars that suppressed any dissenting thought that occurred 200 years after Confucius's death. Therefore, experts have had to use fragments of information to test the reliability of what has been passed down today.

We do know that Confucius wrote many letters about the turmoil of his time. He traveled quite a bit trying to promote virtue and his teachings, but ended up expelled from many places. This is why Confucius is often referred to as "a king without a crown."

It is the Analects of Confucius that are considered the primary source for much of his teaching. It is filled with his sayings, discussions, and thoughts. Still, the Analects are often interpreted in different ways, creating much debate over the meaning of the passages. In his teaching, he uses much more rhetoric, analogy, and aphorism to convey concepts that were very contextualized which often adds to the confusion.

© 2012 Breely Crush Publishing, LLC

Classical Confucianism

Classical Confucianism is the trend initiated by Confucius that was then developed by his disciples Mencius (371 – 289 BC) and Hsun-tzu (313 – 238 BC) that culminated in the I-chuan and Chung-yung. The disciples took Confucianism and developed it into an ethical and political doctrine.

The moral philosophy of Confucianism is grounded in the inherited religion of Heaven, or the Lord-on-High. Society is founded on the insight of a wise and sagely mind. Confucianism is not necessarily thought of as a mystical religion, but the Book of Mencius must be looked at with an eye for mysticism.

Classical Confucianism asserts that a sage that has achieved true integrity will become one with the Heaven and the Earth. It gives a heavy emphasis to ethics and human relationships. Confucius believed that it was Heaven itself that protected Confucius and offered him his message. Therefore Confucianism finds a morality in the divine transcendence.

In the Book of Mencius, Mencia creates an image of Confucius as a teacher of mysticism, stating that there is a presence in the heart that is greater than the self. Confucius offered an implicitly religious message, and Mencius makes it explicit. Mencius' teachings create a system of thought around the relationship between the Way of Heaven and human nature, which was not discussed by Confucius. He believed that if human nature was cultivated in the correct manner, then any person could become a sage. The cultivation comes form a harmony between emotional and psychic equilibrium. This harmony allows people to be in touch with the cosmic forces of life and creativity.

Hsun-Tzu focused more on ritual action. He asserts that we must strive to live a life of jen, or perfect humanity. It is in the proper ritual action that transforms the human heart into the mind of a sage. Without ritual, one could not maintain the insights of Confucius or Mencia. It is only when you add the noble humility and graceful conduct to the liturgy of daily life that one fully grasps Confucianism.

Eventually Classical Confucianism gave way to neo-Confucianism, which leans more in the direction of being pantheistic. Pantheistic literally means "God is All" or "All is God". This means that those who are pantheistic believe that God and nature are all one. There is more influence of Taoism and Buddhism now in Confucianism. Neo-Confucianism offers more practical guidance for creating the perfect mind and gaining sagehood either through gradual self-cultivation or an enlightenment experience (depending on which school of thought one subscribes).

© 2012 Breely Crush Publishing, LLC

Major Themes in Confucianism

While there are schools of thought that may vary within Confucianism, there are several common themes throughout the teachings. Confucian thought is significantly grounded in honesty, so elements of that virtue have expanded over time into these themes:

Jen

Jen is someone's goodness, or in Confucian thought, the concept of being humane. To Confucius, individual development took place in the context of human relationships, so he created what we now know as the Golden Rule, "Do not do to others what you would not like them to do to you." While Jen is sometimes seen as a social or filial dimension of Confucianism, it is also has a political focus. If a ruler does not have jen, then his subjects will not have it either. The ruler will then lose the Mandate of Heaven and his seat of power.

Chun

Chun is the word for a perfect man. Confucius taught that all men should strive to be perfect in that they should combine the qualities of a saint, scholar, and gentleman at all times. Even though the term was based on masculine bias, today it is still used even for women. Confucius was thought to have exemplified this concept. In the religion, men are expected to act as a moral guide to others. They were expected to cultivate a morality, perform rituals correctly, show loyalty, and strive for humaneness.

Li

Li is the Chinese term for ritual or to sacrifice in a religious ceremony. It can be used as the term for everyday propriety or politeness, but has been expanded to include secular ceremonial behavior. Rituals in Confucianism are treated as if they are an all-embracing system of norms. Confucius was the authority of ritual behavior and etiquette.

Te

One already knows from Jen that a ruler has the responsibility to be humane. However, "te" is a term most often linked to virtue. A leader must lead by virtue. Te allows a leader to lead and influence others. It gains them respect. It was also believed that if a leader was powerful, his Te could help him overcome death.

Wen

Wen is a Chinese concept referring to the arts of peace, which was held in high esteem by Confucius. Wen consists of music, poetry, and art, and they are symbols of virtue throughout society. Confucius believed that if a person rejected the arts of peace, he was also rejecting the virtue of Heaven.

Heaven

Heaven is an ambiguous theme in Confucianism. In early references like the Analects, it refers to a supreme deity. However later it is referred to as a moral force and then the universe itself.

Filial Piety

A central concept of Confucianism is the relationships between people, so filial piety is essential. There are five cardinal relationships like that between father and son in which the son shows respect toward his father. This later led to the worship of ancestors.

Humanity

The relationship between people is a central theme of Confucianism, as can be seen in filial piety. While juniors should respect elders, elders are expected to also be respectful of juniors, just in different ways. It is still a common theme throughout East Asia today.

 © 2012 Breely Crush Publishing, LLC

CHAPTER 6: Taoism

While Confucianism seeks to perfect people within the world, both in a secular and spiritual way, Taoism is very much its opposite. Taoists prefer to turn away from society, instead becoming fulfilled in a trans-ethical contemplation of nature. One becomes "at one with oneself." There is a quest for freedom from the social constraints present in Confucianism.

Some believe that Taoism is a religion of passive contemplation, but to great Taoist thinker, Lao-tzu and Chuang-tzu encouraged Taoists to transcend the limited existence of the human condition. They wanted to find the mystery of life and steal the secret of Heaven and Earth so that they could become immortal. This striving for immortality is central to Taoism.

Taoist Beliefs and Practices

There are basically two schools of thought within Taoism, and they have some different practices and deities. While Taoism is not necessarily a belief-centered religion, there are some characteristics of each school of thought.

Religious Taoism

Religious Taoism often uses the Daozang, or "Taoist Canon." It contains texts, alchemical texts, and scriptures. Even though it uses the Daozang, it is not like other religions where the writing is primary. Religious Taoists often use texts that have been passed down from teacher to student rather than reading the Daozang.

Religious Taoists believe that there are supernatural beings that belong to various classes. There are Gods, ghosts, and ancestral spirits. The Gods are neither good nor evil. Meanwhile, Taoists put a lot of emphasis on appeasing ghosts and ancestors through rituals. These rituals are necessary to maintain a good relationship with the spirits and Gods, and they often can gain control over these beings with talismans. Also, rituals are used to maintain health and to align oneself with cosmic forces.

Since Religious Taoism is polytheistic, the deities fit into a hierarchy that is similar to that of Ancient China, and deities can be promoted within the hierarchy or demoted.

© 2012 Breely Crush Publishing, LLC

Many of the deities are believed to be virtuous humans once. Geography often determines which deities are worshipped.

In worship, Religious Taoists will often bow toward an altar, which can feature any number of ancestors or deities, with a stick of incense in one hand. This act can be done in a home, temple, or even outdoors. Most worship is done in accordance with specific dates on the Chinese calendar. Sometimes food is set out for the ancestral spirits or they may burn Hell Bank Notes. These notes are simply specially printed monies that are thought to be used by the spirits in the afterlife. As spirits "live on" in the afterlife, they need money to have the same types of conveniences they had in this life. For celebrations, there are also parades, fortune telling, and meditations.

Philosophical Taoism

Philosophical Taoism is not necessarily a philosophy adhered to by a group, but it is a way of reading the Taoist texts including the Dao De Jing and Zhuangzi. It focuses on the themes of Daoism such as non-action, emptiness, detachment, and flexibility. It also looks deeply at receptiveness, spontaneity, human relativism, and behavior. Philosophical Taoists try to answer what Tao is rather than dogma. Therefore, most worship comes in the form of study.

While Religious Taoism focuses on worshipping the deities, Philosophical Taoists are more concerned with the divinity of the Tao than actually worshiping any deity.

Chuang Tzu was a very influential Chinese philosopher. He took Lao Tzu's philosophies and further developed them. He took them from mystical perspectives, and made them transcendental. He believed that life was dynamic and continually changing. Chuang Tzu, Lao Tzu, and many other philosophers' ideas are what shaped Taoism.

Taoist Symbols

There are several symbols that are associated with Taoism like the Taijitu, Laozi, and Bagua.

Taijitu

The Taijitu is most commonly represented as the Yin and Yang. It is the representation of opposing, and yet complementary, forces in all things.

    © 2012 Breely Crush Publishing, LLC

Laozi

Laozi are the Chinese characters that are specific or associated with Taoism.

Bagua

The Bagua is also known as the eight trigrams. It is a basic philosophical concept in Ancient China represented by an octagonal diagram with tone trigram on each side.

Chapter 7: Judaism

Out of the three largest monotheistic religions in the world, Judaism is the oldest. In fact, it is the parent religion to both Christianity and Islam. Judaism is monotheistic in that it believes in only one true God, who created and continues to rule the world. God is both transcendent and eternal. He is omnipotent. In Judaism, the Jewish people are the "Chosen Ones" in that they are to be an example to all others in the world of God's magnificence.

Historical Development of Judaism

Jewish religious history is rather extensive, yet there are some major elements that are important to understanding the development of Judaism from its early formation to the religion we know today. Many of the elements are also essential for understanding the foundation of both Christianity and Islam.

Ancient Judaism

Jews have an extensive religious history that can be traced back to the patriarch Abraham. In Abraham's covenant with God, he moved to Canaan around 1800 BC, and God kept his promise to make Abraham the father of a great nation. Through his sons, Isaac and Jacob, Judaism began. While some historians believe that early Jews believed that there were other Gods, but they viewed their God as the sole Creator of everything. Yaweh, or God to the Jews, was a jealous God and required Jews to worship him alone.

© 2012 Breely Crush Publishing, LLC

By 1600 BC, the Jews migrated to Egypt during a famine. Egypt remained rich with food and water mostly due to the prophecy and dream interpretation of Joseph. After Joseph passed, though, the Pharaoh at the time forgot Egypt's gratitude replacing it with jealousy of the thriving Jews, so he enslaved them. They were held in slavery until 1280 BC when Moses led the people out of Egypt.

While in the desert seeking the land of "milk and honey," otherwise known to Canaan, God gave the Jews the Ten Commandments and many other laws. Through these laws God made a covenant with the Israelites that began the religious tradition inherent in Judaism. Yet it was also during this time that they defied Yahweh, so God made them roam the desert for 40 years prior to letting them enter Canaan around 1200 BC.

Saul then established a kingdom that was then passed on to King David and later Solomon. The capital was in Jerusalem. Yet after the rule of Solomon, the kingdom split in two, establishing the northern kingdom of Israel and the southern kingdom of Judah. In the 8th century BC, Israel was invaded by the Assyrians and conquered. It was not until the 6th century BC that the Babylonian army defeated the kingdom of Judah.

The center of all Jewish worship was the First Temple, and the Babylonians who invaded Judah destroyed it. Meanwhile, the elite of Judah were exiled to Babylonia. During this time the Jews in Babylonia wrote the "Babylonian Talmud" and the Jews that were left in Judea wrote the "Palestinian Talmud," creating the first written form of the Torah and the Talmud used today. Eventually, Persia defeated the Babylonians, and the Jews returned home to build the Second Temple.

The Second Temple Judaism

Now that the Second Temple was built, the Jews were free to resume their religious practices. The Great Assembly was known as the highest religious authority, and it was led by the prophet Ezra. During this time the last books of the Jewish Bible were written and then the canon sealed.

In 66 AD the Jews revolted against Rome and the Second Temple was destroyed. Only the Western Wall of it still remained. A second revolt occurred, and Jews were not only forbidden to enter the city, but Jewish worship was banned by Rome. It was a result of this ban that Jewish worship was no longer Temple centered. Jews substituted prayer for sacrifice. Rabbis became teachers and leaders in communities, and worship was built around their teachings.

 © *2012 Breely Crush Publishing, LLC*

Modern Judaism

By the first century AD, several Jewish sects arose known as the Pharisees, Sadducees, Zealots, Essenes, and Christians, but they dissipated with the destruction of the Second Temple. While Christianity survived, it broke from Judaism to become its own religion. Pharisees became Rabbinic Judaism that is practiced today under the simple name "Judaism."

The Sadducees, however, relied on the Torah as being the only divinely inspired writing, disregarding the Prophets and other writings. There were also other Jews that denied the oral authority of the Pharisees recorded in the Mishnah. These Jews relied on the Tanakh. This group formed the Karaite sect of Judaism. They are currently still active in small numbers. Karaite and Rabbinical Jews both agree that each sect is Jewish, but they claim the other's faith is mistaken.

Today there are a number of different ethic groups of Jews like the Ashkenazi Jews of Central and Eastern Europe and the Sephardi Jews of Spain, Portugal, and North Africa. There are minor differences in practice based mostly on cultural differences rather than doctrinal disputes. Out of 5.1 million Jews in the U.S. 4.3 million report a continuing connection with the religion. The Jewish leaders, however, worry about the decreasing Jewish population due to intermarriage and assimilation. However, Jewish leaders have added new ways to approach Jewish worship that have increased its popularity of late.

Persecutions

Jews are no strangers to persecution. Throughout the Bible, neighboring countries persecuted Jews, usually coinciding with corruption within the society. By the Middle Ages, there was a great amount of Anti-Semitism (hatred of Jews) that resulted in persecution, pogrom, forced conversion, social restriction, and placements in ghettos. This new persecution had no political motivation, but now persecution was based more on theology and the Christian view of Judaism.

Diaspora
The Jewish Diaspora began around the 8th-6th century BC with the conquest of Israel and Judah. Diaspora is the term which describes the forced expulsion of Jews from what later became the State of Israel. The Diaspora includes the destruction of the First Temple, Second Temple, Roman occupation, and times of slavery. When the State of Israel was officially established in 1948, the term evolved to describe any Jewish person living outside the State of Israel.

© 2012 Breely Crush Publishing, LLC

Expulsion from Spain

Prior to 1492, Spain contained the largest Jewish settlement in Europe. However, Ferdinand and Isabella first drove out the Muslim Moors, then the Jews. It was said that the expulsion was a result of a strong nationalism, but it is also believed that Queen Isabella had a religious zeal that demanded the 53,000 Jewish families be driven out of the country within three months of the edict. Some Jews negotiated an agreement to stay, but they had to pay a large sum of money. Still, Queen Isabella's belief that God demanded the Jews be driven out prevailed, and the remainder had to leave the country. Not only were they expelled, but they also had to exchange all of their gold and silver for cloth and skin, as Jews were forbidden to export any precious metals. The crews also robbed the Jews that got on ships to leave. The term Sephardim or Sephardi is used to encompass descendants of Jews who left Spain in the 15th century. Today there are around 12,000 Jews living in Spain.

The Holocaust

The massive genocide that occurred during World War II is one of the black marks on human history. Millions of Jews were imprisoned and murdered under Nazi rule. They were persecuted solely on the fact that they were Jewish. The fact that a large number of Jews died in the Holocaust created a demographic shift, which changed the religion into the organized Judaism most people know today. Yom HaShoah was even added to the Jewish calendar to remember the Jews that died in the Holocaust.

Major Themes of Judaism

There are themes that run through Judaism back through its beginning when God made his covenant with Abraham. These themes are covered in the remainder of this chapter.

Nature of God

Jews accept God's existence without question. Yahweh, or I am, is the creator of the entire universe. Jews do not know who God is or how He is created. When Moses asked Him for His name, God said for Moses to tell the people, "I am sent me." God is viewed as the one and only God. He is the only one deserving of praise. He is also incorporeal, meaning that he has no body, despite terms like "The Hand of God" or "God walking in the Garden of Eden." Yahweh is believed to be in all places at all times, and it is believed that He can do anything. Yahweh is another name for the God of Abraham, Isaac, and Jacob. It can be translated many different ways, such as "I will be what I want to be," or "I am that I am," or "I am He that causes to be" (Creator). The Jews consider this word to be too sacred to pronounce, so whenever they come to it they instead say "Adonai" which means Lord.

God gave the people free will, so He cannot compel Jews to do His will. He believes that it is the ultimate sign of love of Him that the Jews worship and live according to His laws, because they are choosing to do so rather than being forced to worship Him. Jews believe that God gave them free will, because He is a just and merciful God. Even though God passed judgment on the Jews for their corruption and disobedience, He always lifted the discipline when they repented.

Jews also believe that God is omniscient and eternal. He has no beginning and no end, and He can see into the past, present, and future of everyone's minds. Also, God is perfect and holy, and is often referred to as such by His many names.

Covenant

A major foundation of the Jewish religion is the covenant, or agreement, between God and His people. There are several covenants that are explained in the Hebrew Bible. The first covenant was made between God and Noah in Genesis. God was going to destroy all the people of the Earth, because they were so corrupted and sinful. However, Noah was a good man, and God decided to allow him to live. After the Great Flood, God promised Noah that He would not destroy all mankind again. This covenant is symbolized by a rainbow.

The second covenant occurs between God and Abraham, in which God agrees to make Abraham the father of a great nation and to give them the land of Israel. He promises Abraham these things as long as Abraham lives an obedient life. The symbol of this covenant is the circumcision.

The third covenant is the one between God and the Israelites after the Exodus when they are at Mt. Sinai. God makes his promise that Israel will become a special possession among all nations. He gives the Israelites the Ten Commandments as their obligations. This covenant is based on God's grace, as God maintains both sides of the covenant.

Later, God also makes a more personal covenant with David. God promises to keep David's descendants on the throne for all time as long as he follows God's conditions.

Abraham

According to the Bible, Abraham was commanded by El-Shaddai (a Jewish name for God) to sacrifice his son Isaac. He was ready to perform the sacrifice when God intervened and allowed the substitution of a ram for his son. He was promised his descendants would have a permanent home in the Land of Canaan. He was also told that he would be known as Father of many nations. After his death, his place was taken by first his son Isaac, then his grandson Jacob.

Talmud

Jewish law was originally an oral tradition, but around 70 AD they decided that a written law would be needed. This became the Talmud, a book second only to the Hebrew Bible in Judaism. The two major components of the Talmud are the Mishnah and Gemara. Mishnah means repetition. This section is broken down into several smaller sections. It is a large work containing references to the legal decisions of rabbis in the past. Gemara means completion. This section is basically a commentary on the Mishnah.

Torah

God's revelation of His divine intention is also known as the Torah, which is the law in Judaic scriptures. It is the single most important text in Judaism. The Pentateuch, or first five books of the Hebrew Bible are those that make up the Torah. The books are as follows: Genesis, Exodus, Leviticus, Numbers, and Deuteronomy. Through the Torah, the Jewish people are given practical guidance in relation to God's principles and their everyday life. The instructions of the Torah are presented to the Jewish people in the form of a gift, but at the same time, they come with a warning of God's judgment if the Jews are disobedient.

Traditionally, the Torah was taken as the literal word that God gave to Moses on Mount Sinai. It guides the relationship between God and man and gives the Jews a sense of purpose in that relationship.

The Torah contains 613 mitzvot or "commandments." Much of Genesis, along with a portion of Numbers and Exodus are story-related. However, the remainder is mostly law-driven. The stories are important, because they put the law into context for the

 © 2012 Breely Crush Publishing, LLC

Jewish people. Deuteronomy, though, remains different, because it Moses' final speeches to the Israelites before he passes away.

Sometimes the Torah is written on a scroll that is used for rituals. A lot of care and methodology is used in creating these scrolls, and some have been found that are centuries old. To a Jew, every word in the Torah has a divine meaning, so great care must be taken so that no marking is inadvertently changed. Torah scrolls are always stored in the holiest parts of the synagogue, or Holy Ark, showing the Jews reverence for the Word of God.

Prophecy

While today we mostly define prophets as those who can see the future, to a Jew there is much more to prophet than that ability. To a Jew, a prophet is a person who is chosen by God to speak for God as exemplified in the Jewish word for prophet, navi, or fruit of the lips. The Jewish prophets were role models to the people. They lived lives of holiness, scholarship, and worship that others were to emulate.

The Hebrew Bible names 55 prophets. There was no sexual discrimination in who could or could not be a prophet. Several of the prophets were women. In fact, it was told that Sarah's ability to prophesy was greater than Abraham's. Also, a person need not even be a Jew to be a prophet. Some prophets, like Jonah, were even sent on missions to preach God's word to the Gentiles, or non-Jews.

Prophecy is considered by Jews to be a gift given by God. It is not arbitrarily given, but offered if one develops the right spirituality and strong ethics. However, if a prophet does wrong, the gift can be taken. The story of Jonah and the whale is an example of a prophet-gone-wrong that loses his ability due to his sin.

The greatest prophet of the Hebrew Bible is Moses. It is widely believed that Moses saw all of what other prophets saw and more. He saw the entire Torah, even parts that were to be written after his death.

Rituals

While Jews have prayer times and say different prayers in worship, there are also several holidays and rituals that are considered ordained by God.

Shabbat

Shabbat is considered the Sabbath day. When God created the earth, men, and animals, he rested on the seventh day. He commanded that men do the same. Shabbat begins at sundown on Friday night to just after sundown on Saturday night. In Judaism, all work activities are forbidden during this time, and there are 39 categories of work.

Passover

Passover is a week-long holiday commemorating the Exodus from Egypt. God commanded that the Jews celebrate Passover to remind them of His grace in releasing them from their bondage. They may not eat any leaven bread, nor can they have any in the house. There is the Seder, or home service, where everyone gathers to celebrate. A traditional Seder meal includes the shank bone, bitter herbs, and parsley – all which have symbolic meaning.

Shavuot

Shavuot also goes by the names Pentecost and Feast of Weeks. It is a celebration of Moses giving the Ten Commandments to the Israelites.

Rosh Hashanah

Rosh Hashanah is one of the high holy days. While the name means "New Year," it actually occurs in the seventh month of the Hebrew calendar. It is a celebration of the world's creation and begins the atonement period that ends in Yom Kippur. A Jew is expected to apologize to everyone he or she has wronged over the past year during Rosh Hashanah.

Yom Kippur

Yom Kippur is a day of atonement in which Jews fast for past sins, whether individual or communal. Jews consider this day the most important Jewish holiday.

Purim

In the book of Esther, the Persian Jews were delivered by near annihilation. During this holiday, the Jews give gifts, eat and drink, and read from the Book of Esther.

Hanukkah

Hanukkah, or the Festival of Lights, is not a Jewish holiday described in the Hebrew Bible, but it is one of the most recognized holidays by outsiders. Hanukkah is eight days long and commemorates the Maccabees victory over the Seleucid Empire at the Second Temple. While there was only enough consecrated oil to burn the eternal flame for one day, it miraculously lasted eight days. The eight days is what it took to make new oil. The holiday is celebrated by lighting candles each night, playing dreidel games, and eating foods fried in olive oil.

© 2012 Breely Crush Publishing, LLC

Bar Mitzvah

Bar Mitzvah is translated to mean *a son of the commandments*. In the Jewish tradition, when a boy turns 13, he officially enters the community as an adult. The boy is called a Bar Mitzvah (which is also the name of the ceremony). As a celebration of this, there is a Bar Mitzvah ceremony in which the boy "leads public worship" to demonstrate his status. The boy is now responsible for all of the obligations and observances of a religious adult.

Symbols

There are several symbols used to represent different aspects or rituals in Judaism.

The Star of David

The Star of David is the major symbol of the Jewish people. It consists of two triangles, one pointing up and one down, overlapped. The symbol was not actually used to signify the Jews until the Middle Ages. There are many theories as to the development of the Star of David from the significance of the number six to the astrological chart at the time of David's birth.

The Prayer Shawl

The Tallit is the Jewish prayer shawl. It is only worn during morning services, the Torah service, and on Yom Kippur. The fringes on the ends, or tzitzit, are knotted and twisted in a special way. The Tallit is a special possession often passed down from generation to generation. The more threadbare it becomes from use, the more respected it becomes.

Yarmulke

The yarmulke, or kippah, is a common site in Judaism. It is a round skullcap that is worn by Jews, most often during service. While the yarmulke is traditionally worn by men, recently it is sometimes worn by women in more non-orthodox settings.

Menorah

Before the 16th century AD, the menorah was the primary symbol of Judaism. It is a seven-branched candelabra used in the Tabernacles. Its shape symbolizes the burning bush on Mount Sinai. It is most closely associated with the Jewish holiday Hanukkah.

Worship

There are three main prayer services each day, the Shacharit, Mincha, and Maariv. They each include benedictions called the Amidah, and the number of benedictions varies on whether it is a weekday or holy day. The Shema is a declaration of faith. If there are not at least ten people present it is not an actual prayer service, but a prayer quorum.

Zionism

The extreme anti-Semitism of the 19th century convinced many Jews that the only hope for security lay in creating a home in Palestine. This view was strengthened with Theodor Herzl's book The Jewish State, published in 1896. Herzl is considered the founder of Zionism because based on this book, a movement called Zionism began to gain support. The first sect to embrace Zionism was the Orthodox Jews. During WWI, the British government announced that they viewed this course of action favorably, and over the next twenty years thousands of Jews made their way to Palestine to lay the foundation of their new home.

Modern Judaism

Reconstructionalist Sect
The Reconstructionalist sect of Judaism began as a part of the conservative sect and branched off. It was founded by Rabbi Mordecai Kaplan in the 1920's through 1940's. The basis of the sect is that it isn't really possible to adhere to all of the laws as were believed anciently, due to advances in science, philosophy and technology.

A Get
In Hebrew, a divorce granted by a rabbi is called a get. In Jewish Law, a husband must present his wife with a get before they are considered divorced. Essentially, the wife is no longer a married women, and she is returned the legal rights which the husband held in marriage. Because she is no longer married, the laws of adultery no longer apply.

Kabbala
Hebrew is a complex language in which letters of the alphabet also stand for numbers. The Kabbala is a system of theology which interprets the scriptures using different interpretations of number symbolisms, and arrangements of words and numbers. This results in hidden, deeper meaning to the scriptures.

 © 2012 Breely Crush Publishing, LLC

CHAPTER 8: Christianity

While Judaism is one of the oldest and largest monotheistic religion, its numbers cannot compare to those of its offshoot, Christianity. In 2001 it was believed that were at least 2.1 billion Christians, which made it the world's largest religion then, and it continues to grow. It is an Abrahamic religion like Judaism and Islam, and much of its foundation can be seen in the Old Testament. It began in the 1st century as a Jewish sect, yet broke off from Judaism to form its own religion.

There are several denominations in Christianity with their own traditions and church bodies. However, whether someone belongs to the branch of Roman Catholicism, Eastern Orthodoxy, or Protestantism, there is a common foundation of beliefs. It is only in the doctrinal differences of custom and place that vary in the branches of Christianity.

Historical Development of Christianity

Christianity is monotheistic, as they believe that there is one God that created the universe and holds power over it. Where it differs from Judaism is in the idea of the Christ, or Messiah. In early Judaism, messiah was used to name any person appointed as a prophet of God. However, there were numerous Jewish prophecies of a "savior" that would deliver them from their problems with the Romans. The Christian sect, though, believed that this "savior" was to be a spiritual savior.

According to Christian belief, this messiah was associated with numerous prophecies in the Hebrew Bible. He was to be a descendent of David, and would be the new Leader of the Jews. He would rebuild Israel, bring world peace, destroy the evil, and judge the world. Within those prophecies, the Messiah was to be one with God, or he is the God of Abraham, Isaac, and Jacob. He was to die and make atonement for the sins of the people and serve as an example of Godliness to the people.

Christians assert that Jesus of Nazareth fulfilled the prophecies laid out in the Hebrew Bible, or Old Testament, and therefore is the Christ. They believe he will return to fulfill the remainder during the Second Coming. This view is controversial among Jews and Islam, as there were also many warnings of false prophets. However Christians assert that, as Jesus fulfilled all the prophecies of a Messiah, he is the One True Christ.

© 2012 Breely Crush Publishing, LLC

The Life of Jesus

Jesus of Nazareth is the central figure of Christianity. The Gospel of Matthew has the most detailed account of Jesus' birth and life. While there is no exact date of his birth, there is also debate over the circumstances. In the Book of Matthew, it is said that an angel descended a young Jewish woman named Mary, who was then engaged to a man named Joseph. The angel told Mary that she was going to give birth to a boy, who she should name "Jesus," thus fulfilling the prophecy of the virgin birth. In Jewish tradition, virgin birth was not that uncommon, so it was not as questionable as it is to people today.

Much is told of the birth of Jesus in the Nativity. Herod the Great demanded that they return to Joseph's home for the census, and there was no room at the inn. Therefore, Jesus was born in a manger in Bethlehem. It is important to understand that Jesus was born and raised as a Jew. He lived out his life as a Jew, which is important later when he is faced with temptations and confrontation. Although Jesus was born in Bethlehem, lived for a time in Egypt, and preached in Jerusalem, most of his life was spent in Nazareth.

Throughout the four gospels, which tell the stories of Jesus' life, there is little said about his life between his infancy and the age of twelve. As an infant, his family fled to Egypt to protect him from being killed at the command of King Herod. Nothing else is told until the Finding in the Temple later.

In the Gospel of Luke, Jesus and his family went on pilgrimage to Jerusalem. When his parents left, Jesus stayed behind in the Temple to debate with the religious teachers, though Mary and Joseph did not realize it. He was there three days when his worried parents returned for him. When they admonished him, he replied, "Why were you searching for me...Didn't you know that I had to be in my Father's house?"

A significant figure in Jesus' life is John the Baptist. He was born to Elisabeth about six months before the birth of Jesus, and it was said that he would be a prophet that would "prepare the way for the Lord." John had a ministry near the Jordan River where he preached of the coming Lord. Jesus comes to John and asks him to conduct a baptism. Prior to this moment, Jesus did not have a ministry. When Jesus was baptized, it is said that the heavens opened up and the "Spirit of God" descended on Jesus in the form of a dove. A voice announces that this is God's beloved son and God is well pleased with him. Critics ask why Jesus had to be baptized when he was sinless, but Christians believe that he was baptized so that humanity knows it is important and it allowed him to take on the burden of humanity's sin.

© 2012 Breely Crush Publishing, LLC

After his baptism, Jesus went out into the desert where it is believed that he faced temptation by Satan. He fasted for 40 days and nights in the desert, and Satan continuously tempted Jesus to demonstrate his divinity in a supernatural manner. Jesus used the Word of God as written in Deuteronomy. After Satan failed in tempting Jesus, he left and it is said that angels descended on Jesus to offer him nourishment.

Jesus then left the desert and began his ministry. The people of the time were astounded when Jesus took on disciples from the less-than-desirable parts of humanity like tax collectors and fishermen. Around 30 AD, Jesus gave one of his great sermons named, "The Sermon on the Mount." In this sermon he gave the Beatitudes and the Lord's Prayer, which are common in religious practices today. Also, he told the people of the Golden Rule, which is similar to the Confucian belief that one should not do to others what they would not want done to them. For many Christians, it is believed that the Sermon on the Mount was a commentary on the Ten Commandments. It contains the central beliefs of Christianity.

Jesus went on to appoint the twelve Apostles and perform many exorcisms and sermons. The transfiguration of Jesus upon a mountain in front of Peter, John, and James was a significant act to demonstrate his divinity. Jesus also returned to Jerusalem, where he became upset with the exchange of blessed money for coinage of the Greeks and Romans. He chastised the money changes for making the Temple a "den of thieves." It is after this act that the Pharisees and Sadducees began to plot against Jesus.

During this time, Jesus talks a lot of his death, the destruction of the Temple, and Tribulation. While Jesus is clear on what he is saying, much of it remains a mystery to his followers. At the Last Supper, Jesus shared his last meal with his apostles in what is believed by some to be the Passover Seder, though some scholars disagree with the timing. At the Last Supper, Jesus made a new covenant and laid the basis for the Eucharist practiced by Catholics. Jesus talked of his ultimate betrayal by the apostle Judas and his death and resurrection.

Upon Jesus' betrayal, he is put to trial by the Sanhedrin, where he is uncooperative. They cannot find a reason to condemn Jesus to death under the Law, so the Gospels state that they brought forth false witnesses. He was brought to Pontius Pilate for a trial in which Pilate was to determine if Jesus was a political threat. Pilate understood the politics of the day, so he allowed the Jews to make a choice between Jesus and Barabbas, another prisoner. This was the custom of Passover for the Jews to free one prisoner. It was said in the Gospels that the hearts of the Jews were hardened and they freed Barabbas instead. This forces Pilate to condemn Jesus to crucifixion.

There is still considerable debate about who is actually responsible for the condemnation of Jesus. Some place the blame on the Jews, while others place it on Pilate, for Pilate was not known to be a gentle leader. His reputation for cruelty was widely acknowledged, and it was not hard to believe that he would have put Jesus to death to calm the rising tension in the Jewish community.

Jesus was then flogged, beaten, cajoled and hung on the cross. Crucifixion was not a pleasant way to die, and the position of the body caused asphyxiation. It was not uncommon for the legs of the crucified to be broken to speed up death, but this did not occur in Jesus' account. It is said that when he died there was darkness and the veil of the temple split in half. His last words were reported to be, "My God, My God, why have you forsaken me?"

After his death, he was taken from the cross, bound, and placed in a tomb. The tomb was sealed with a great stone and guarded by Roman soldiers to prevent anyone from stealing the body. According to the scripture, three days later there was a great quake, and Mary found the tomb open and empty. Two angels appeared to her and said "why seek ye the living among the dead? He is not here, but is risen." The resurrection narrative in Mark is hotly debated among experts, yet the book of Acts and 1 Corinthians both offer a resurrection as the cornerstone of Christianity.

When Mary tells the men of the missing body and Jesus' resurrection, they do not believe her. It is after this point that Jesus makes appearances to the disciples until he rises to Heaven to remain until the Second Coming. There are many disputes over the validity of the resurrection. Some critics believe the body was stolen, that Jesus was not really dead when he was taken from the cross, that the post-resurrection Jesus was a hallucination, that the Jesus who died on the cross was not really Jesus, and that Judas died in his place. However, to devout Christians, there is no doubt that Jesus exhibited his power over life and death in the resurrection.

The Early Church to the Medieval Church

The early church, in the first 40 years after Jesus' resurrection, was more like a Jewish sect. This church opened up its doors to non-Christians and did not even require them to be circumcised. In 70 AD, Jerusalem fell to the Romans, and the Christians had to disperse. Over the next two hundred years the Christians were subject to great persecution. Yet even during this persecution, the central church held to the belief that their faith was given by Christ to the apostles and handed down to all humanity.

In 312, the church faced a turning point in the relationship with the Roman Empire when Emperor Constantine converted to Christianity. This led to a long line of Roman emperors that were almost all Christian and also taking the Christian church from a state of persecution to one of favor.

Over several centuries, there were disagreements that occurred in the church, causing the eventual breach between the Roman Catholic Church and the Eastern Orthodox Church. It was not a violent breach, as would occur between the Roman Catholic Church and Protestants later, but it gradually occurred over a period of time.

It was during the Medieval Era the role of the church was great. People were terrified of Hell, and they were told that the only way they could get to Heaven was if the Church let them. Clergy had become dominant, and they alone actively participated in worship. It was believed that Christ gave them the priesthood and the abilities to turn bread and wine into the body and blood of Christ. Mass was held in Latin, but the common people could not understand it. People also did not receive communion except for special occasions like Easter.

A group of people took a stand against what they thought were abuses of the church. These reformers wanted to return to God's Word and move away from ritual toward an understanding of doctrine. They took the power of getting to heaven away from priest and their deeds and returned it to the idea that the belief in Jesus as the Way would get them to Heaven. Hymn singing and sermons were added to church life.

The Eastern Orthodox Church

The Eastern Orthodox Churches are a group that shares an ethos from the Byzantine Empire. The Eastern Orthodox Church is spread across Eastern Europe, the Slav nations, and the eastern Mediterranean. It consists of several factions such as the Greek Orthodox Church, Armenian Orthodox Church, and Coptic Orthodox Church. It claims to be the original Christian Church as founded by Christ and His Apostles.

The Eastern Orthodox Church broke off form the Roman Catholic through disagreements that occurred over centuries. It is differs from the other branches of Christianity in that it has the Divine Liturgy, Sacraments, and the preservation of tradition. They are jurisdiction based and self-governed. They also reject the papal claim of supreme authority.

© 2012 Breely Crush Publishing, LLC

Differences between the Roman Catholic Church and the Eastern Orthodox Church

Since the Great Schism in the 11th century, differences have developed between the Roman Catholic and Eastern Orthodox Churches. Both churches believe in baptism and original sin, however they have different interpretations of the effects of original sin. The Roman Catholic Church believes in the authority of the Pope. The Pope is considered infallible and has complete superiority over all other leaders. In Orthodoxy, there is no Pope (although there is the highest bishop, called the "first among equals"), and the bishops and leaders are not considered infallible or given total authority. The Eastern Orthodox church does not believe in purgatory and icons are essential. Eastern Orthodox priests can get married prior to ordination, and Roman Catholic bishops cannot get married.

Gospel

In Christianity, the term "gospel" means "good news." It can be used to describe the spoken word of Jesus, a hypothetical genre of early Christian literature, or the first four books of the New Testament. Paul used the term when he was preaching to the men of Corinth as documented in 1 Corinthians 15:1.

The canonical books of the New Testament are known as the Gospels of Matthew, Mark, Luke, and John. The first three are known as the Synoptic Gospels, as they relate their stories in very similar ways. It is their similarities that have created the Synoptic problem, or the debate over the validity of the Gospels. Some believe that the Gospels are the Word of God, written by God, which is why they are so similar. Others believe it is the result of three people reporting the same event.

There are other written gospels that have not been accepted into the canon, because there are doubts of their authorship. Some are accepted by small sects of Christians, but most mainstream Christian churches consider their use heretical. The Gospel of Thomas is considered one of the more controversial non-canonical gospels.

© 2012 Breely Crush Publishing, LLC

Paul

Paul, also known as St. Paul, was responsible for the Pauline Epistles. The Pauline Epistles are the 13 books in the New Testament ranging from Romans to Titus. Therefore his influence in Christian thinking is greater than basically any others. Paul was from Tarsus (which is why he is also known as Paul of Tarsus). Along with Simon Peter and James the Just, Paul is considered to be one of the most notable leaders of the early church.

Stephen

Stephen was a disciple of Christ and is considered to be the first Christian martyr. After Christ's death he continued to preach about him and was put on trial for blasphemy. At the trial he accused the judges of being murderers of the Son of God. The angry crowd took him into the road and he was stoned. For this, he is considered the first Christian martyr. He was the first to die because of his beliefs.

Sadducees

The Sadducees were generally members of the wealthy, aristocratic class. Basically, the Sadducees were religious, political and governmental leaders all in one. They considered themselves to have a more "reasonable" view of the world then the people. However, their opinions were often seen as being clouded by their many roles. To the Sadducees, anything which created religious unrest or economic instability was frowned upon. Therefore religious innovation was a threat, while cultural innovations to improve relationships abroad were welcomed. They distanced themselves from the needs and wants of the masses, and looked solely at keeping the status quo. They believed that the Books of Moses should be taken literally.

Resurrection

The Christian concept of resurrection is born out of Jewish beliefs. While Jesus did not always agree with the Pharisees, they did agree in this aspect. Christians believe that there is an afterlife, and there will be a resurrection of the dead at the end of time. In the

New Testament, there are several examples of Jesus showing his power over life and death by resurrecting people. One of the greatest examples of this power is the story of how Jesus resurrected Lazarus after his being buried for four days.

 # *Rituals*

There are many rituals associated with Christianity. Some are common rituals to all branches of Christianity, while others are specific to one branch:

Baptism

The baptism is basically a water purification ritual used by Christians to symbolize the washing away of sins as a result of union with Christ. Most Christian's branches practice baptism, though there are some disagreements as to the meaning and power of the baptism itself as well as its form. For some Christian groups there is just a sprinkling of water, while others have a full body immersion.

Eucharist

The Eucharist is also known as communion. It is performed as a result of when Jesus broke the bread at the Last Supper saying, "This is my body," and then drank the wine saying, "This is my blood." While most Christian groups agree that there is a special presence of Christ in the Eucharist, they do not all agree on how and where he is present.

Rites of Passage

Common rites of passage in the Christian Church involve marriage and funeral rites. These vary among different branches of Christianity, but the rites themselves remain common.

Rosary

The rosary is actually a set of prayer beads primarily used by members of the Roman Catholic Church, but the Anglican and Lutheran Churches also use them. A Christian uses prayer and meditation with the beads reciting the Lord's Prayer followed by ten "Hail Mary" prayers.

Seven Sacraments

The Catholic Church has seven sacraments: Baptism, Confirmation, Eucharist (communion), Reconciliation (confession), Anointing of the sick, Matrimony, and Holy Orders. It is not required that every person receives every sacrament, however, in the general sense it is believed that the sacraments are necessary for salvation. Each has its own purpose and if the person receiving the sacrament doesn't have the right attitude, it reduces the effectiveness of the person. The sacraments build, nourish, and strengthen faith.

 © 2012 Breely Crush Publishing, LLC

Symbols

There are several symbols that are used to identify aspects of the Christian Church:

The Cross
The cross is the primary symbol of Christianity. For Orthodox believers the cross is adorned, while for Protestants it is just a simple cross. It is meant to symbolize the cross upon which Christ died for the world's sins.

The Ichthys
Often referred to as the "Jesus Fish," the ichthys is a symbol that combines two intersecting arcs to form the shape of a fish. In the Roman Empire it was used as a secret symbol that other Christians would easily recognize, but others would not. It is often associated with Jesus' statement that he would make his disciples "fishers of men."

Chi-Rho
Emperor Constantine adopted this symbol for Christianity. It consists of the Greek letters "rho" and "chi," in which chi crosses over the rho. They represent the first two letters of the name Christ.

Worship

Christian worship has changed over the ages. Throughout history it was rooted in liturgy with formal prayers and hymns performed in a specific orders as deemed by rituals. It was mostly based on the Jewish model of having set times per day for specific prayers and specific times of year for certain festivals. To Christians, and their forefathers the Jews, worship is at the core of humanity.

Prayer and hymns today are varied based on the culture and practice of each branch of the church. For instance, with the Reformation, singing became an active form of worship rather than just instrumental music. Eucharist, or communion is a part of Christian worship, though its frequency depends also on the branch of Christian belief.

Much of Christian worship is performed in a public manner with a minister of sorts leading the service. However, Christians also worship though meditation, prayer, study, formal occasions, and more that are performed on a much more personal level.

Ulrich Zwingli was a leader of the Reformation in Switzerland. He was a highly educated priest, and advocated a "return" to the doctrine of the New Testament. He believed that worship should include only things which were commanded. He believed that when Christ said "this is my body" he mean "this signifies my body." He believed it was irrational to believe the sacrament was anything other than symbolic, and that ritual should be at a minimum.

The Great Schism

During the 4th century, there were five main centers of Christianity. They were Antioch, Alexandria, Constantinople, Jerusalem, and Rome. As Islam and Christianity competed, Rome and Constantinople became the main Christian centers. Due to political, cultural, and religious differences, the two powers formally separated in 1054 AD. This event was called the Great Schism, after which the Roman Catholic Church became distinct from the Eastern Orthodox Church.

The Sabbath

According to the Bible, God made the world in six days and on the seventh day he rested. For this reason the Jewish Shabbat (Sabbath) is celebrated on the seventh day of the week, Saturday. However, over time, many religions have come to worship on Sundays. The reason for this is that Christ was crucified on the day before the Sabbath, or Friday. He rose from death on the third day, which would be the day after the Sabbath, or Sunday, the first day of the week. Therefore, over time, many religious activities have come to coincide with Sunday, the first day of the week, instead of Saturday, the last day of the week.

Mormonism

Those belonging to The Chuch of Jesus Christ of Latter-Day Saints are commonly called Mormons based on their belief in the Book of Mormon. These Christians believe that in the years following Christ's death that many important, basic and simple truths were lost from the Gospel. These truths were restored when God and Jesus Christ appeared to Joseph Smith in 1820. Joseph was a deeply religious boy who had great decisions about which church to join. He read the Bible, specifically, James 1:5

"If any of you lack wisdom, let him ask of God, —that giveth to all men liberally, and upbraideth not; and it shall be given him"

Feeling he needed wisdom, he went to a grove of trees to pray. God and Jesus Christ appeared to him, giving him instructions to join none of the churches and other important teachings. This is referred to as The First Vision.

Mormons, or Latter-Day Saints, essentially believe in five different books of scripture. The Old and New Testaments in the Bible are the first two. They also believe in a book called the Book of Mormon. This is a record of the people of ancient America. Its purpose is to confirm the truths taught in the Bible. This book was translated by Joseph Smith and the first copy of the translated work was printed in 1830.

Mormons also have the Doctrine and Covenants. This book compiles revelations which were received by Joseph Smith in the early years of the church. The final book of scripture which the Mormons believe in is the Pearl of Great Price. One record in the Pearl of Great Price is Joseph Smith's translation of Genesis, which is called the Book of Moses.

CHAPTER 9: Islam

Judaism gave birth to two religions. One was Christianity and the other was Islam. Like Christianity and Judaism, Islam is an Abrahamic religion and also monotheistic. The religion is based upon the teachings of Muhammad recorded in the Qur'an, as followers believe in Muhammad as God's final prophet. Believers in Islam are called Muslims.

There are over one billion Muslims, making Islam the second largest religion in the world. Muslims believe that Muhammad received God's final word for humanity and that his teachings will last until the Day of the Resurrection. They believe that the word Muhammad wrote in the Qur'an is flawless and unchangeable and that other religions like Judaism and Christianity have distorted the Word of God in the Hebrew Bible and New Testament. Therefore, the Qur'an is a correction of those errors.

Historical Development of Islam

Islam began in 610 AD with the prophet Muhammad. Prior to Islam, most Arabs were members of nomadic tribes that focused more on human excellence than divinity. Mecca at the time was the center of trade and wealth. It had a sanctuary called the Ka'ba that was a pilgrimage center and the district that surrounded it was sacred. The wealth that was so prominent in Mecca that it created much tension between many of the men.

Life of Muhammad

Muhammad was born around 570 AD in Mecca. His name means "the praised one." It is believed that he can trace his family line as far back as Abraham. Early in his life he was orphaned, but learned the importance of having a community surround you. When Muhammad was young he believed in the same religions as the people around him, but as he began to grow up he began looking upon it with a critical eye. He didn't agree with the polytheism (belief in multiple deities/Gods) and animism that he saw. He began to be influenced by the few Christians in his life. By 25 he was a traveling merchant that would sometimes retreat to the mountains outside Mecca to pray and contemplate. He was not a man that was satisfied by material security. He found questions oppressive and he was often restless.

Muhammad was married first to a woman named Khadijah, his only wife from 595 to 619 AD when she died. He later married many other women, totaling 11. He had four daughters and one son with Khadijah. His number of wives exceeded the four dictated by the Qur'an, and it has come under great criticism.

When he was around 40, he believed that he was given messages from God through the Angel Gabriel and that he was to give these messages to the people of Mecca. Later the messages were collected and written in the Qur'an.

As Muhammad began to question the Meccan religion, he came to agree with the belief that there would be a final judgment and punishment of the wicked. These beliefs agree with both Christian and Jewish philosophy. Muhammad received his revelation from the Angel Gabriel being sent by Allah, the same God that the Christians and Jews already believed in. Additionally, the Quran was essentially "further" revelation from Allah. Many Muslims believe that if Muhammad had not known the material of the Old and New Testament, he wouldn't have been able to understand the revelation he received. Because of all these things, Muhammad accepted Christianity and Judaism as parallel religions.

Even though Muhammad had several followers, the people of Mecca did not always receive his messages well. He preached that Allah was "One" and there was going to be a Day of Judgment in which Allah would judge all humanity for their deeds. His preaching went on to tell people to use their wealth well. The merchants of Mecca were resistant to the words that criticized their practices.

Muhammad was preparing to establish himself in Yathrib (Medina) where the leaders had been preparing the people for the arrival of the Prophet. As the time drew nearer

© *2012 Breely Crush Publishing, LLC*

the Meccans heard of the situation and the Quyrash determined to strike quickly. Muhammad and Abu Bakr escaped on camels.

By 622, Muhammad and his followers were being severely persecuted by the people of Mecca, including some of their own relatives, so they fled to Medina. This emigration is known as the Hijra. Medina was a land divided into warring groups. They were receptive to Muhammad who promised to help the groups resolve their differences. Many of the Jewish inhabitants would not recognize him as a prophet of God, so he drove them out and set out to destroy them. This migration is considered to be the birth of Islam.

During this time, the people of Mecca began attacking Medina to destroy Islam. Despite the large numbers of the Meccan army, Medina was able to defeat the Meccans each time. Eventually, Medina invaded Mecca and took control over the city without any blood being shed. The Ka'ba was cleansed of idols and the townspeople accepted Islam. When Mecca finally capitulated, much of the Arabian Peninsula came under Muhammad's authority.

In 632 Muhammad led the hajj from Medina to Mecca. He declared that he had completed the religion for the people and that he had fulfilled his favor toward the people. He expressed his desire for them to adopt Islam as their religion and was leaving them the Book of Allah. When he returned to Medina later that year he died.

The Ka'bah is a shrine located in Mecca. The legend is that a meteor landed in Arabia, and Mecca's awed inhabitants worshipped it, calling it "the black stone that fell from heaven in the days of Adam". Since that time Muslims have gone on pilgrimages for the chance to circle this stone seven times, and kiss it in hopes of heaven's blessing. All praying is directed toward it, nothing is allowed to cross in the column of air above it, and no unclean activity is allowed to take place facing toward it.

Formation of Ummah

Ummah is the Arabic word for community. Often it is used to describe the collective action of Islamic states. In Islam, it is used to describe the community of believers. In the Qur'an there is a reference to "umma wahida" which discusses unifying the Islamic world, which describes the goal of Islam.

Expansion of the Community

Muhammad sought to expand the community of Islam outside of Mecca and Medina. For a century after the taking of Mecca, Islam spread westward, spreading from North Africa to the Atlantic. While not everyone became Muslim, the inhabitants of defeated regions became protected minorities. Islam spread over Persia and Afghanistan and into central Asia. These were mostly military expeditions.

After 750 AD, the military expansion slowed, and Islam's only movement was into India. At this point, there was a climax in Islamic power and it slowed down after this point. However, in about 1500 AD, Islam began a new era in European influence on the eastern Muslims. There were many advances in Europe in technology, and many of the eastern Muslims wanted to share in the comfort and convenience.

Muslims began adopting Western method of teaching and use of new technology. Western people often exploited the Muslims when their rich oil deposits were first discovered. Yet Muslims soon learned the power that oil would bring them in world politics.

Sunni

The Sunni are the largest group of Muslims. While both the Sunnis and Shi'a see Muhammad as a perfect example, and they have to imitate his words and acts as accurately as they can, the two sects disagree on the first three caliphs. Sunnis hold to four legal traditions - Maliki, Shafi'I, Hanafi, and Hanbali. They believe that there is no person who could succeed Muhammad in his nature and prophetic ability. Therefore, they believe that the leader can only be the guardian of the prophetic legacy, or a caliph. Sunnis and Shi'a often clash, as many Sunnis see Shi'a as heretics.

Shi'a

Shi'a Muslims are the second largest branch of Islam. They believe that leaderships should not be passed down through the caliphate, but descendents of Muhammad should be given the right to lead as Imams. A majority of Shi'a live in Iran, and they believe that the cycle of Wilaya will end when the twelfth imam's messianic return. The ayatollah is the highest "doctor of the law." These doctors have access to the twelfth imam's guidance, and they can be seen if a believer needs that guidance.

© 2012 Breely Crush Publishing, LLC

Sunni vs. Shiites

There are two basic branches which emerged after Muhammad's death, however most Muslims don't prefer to classify themselves into one or the other group. Rather they just call themselves Muslim. 90% of the world's Muslim's are Sunnis. The Sunnis believe that the first four caliphs (Muhammad's successors, which the Shiites call Imams) were legitimate leaders and so are their heirs.

The two countries with the highest percentages of Shiites are Iran and Iraq. 50% of the world's Shiites live in either Iran or Iraq. The Shiites believe that only the heirs of the fourth caliph, Ali, are legitimate leaders. They even curse the other four, Abu Bakr, 'Umar, and 'Uthman, in their Friday prayers.

While the initial differences between the two groups were political, over time the two have grown apart in worship as well. One difference is the belief in the Imam (or aman). Shiites believe that the Imam is sinless and perfect, and they sometimes pilgrimage to the tombs of Imams for divine guidance. Basically, the Imam is their leader. Sunnis believe that there is no hereditary base for spiritual leaders, but that it is an earned position.

Sufism

Sufism is the inner spiritual life of both the Sunni and Shi'a. Sufis do not make up a distinct group of Muslims, but they are simply Muslims and can belong to either Sunni or Shi'a groupings. They seek an intimacy with Allah through spiritual purification and discipline. They wish to perfect their faith and shed their egos.

Modern Islam

Fundamentalist Islam is the most prominent movement in recent times, though there is a liberal movement that tries to bring together the strict Islamic beliefs with the questions facing people today. The fundamentalist movement seeks to free Islam from misinterpretation so that Islam will be seen as the center of modern thought and freedom. Much of the need for fundamentalism is that much of the Arab world, where Islam is the major religion, is very oil rich and has to face dealings with the capitalistic world around them. Also, many young people have lost faith in their own society. Fundamentalist Islam offers these people hope and change.

The most resistant to reform is family law. It was not until 1915 that the woman's right to divorce was recognized. Today there is a restriction on polygamy and laws to prevent abuses.

Still, one of the greatest changes occurred in the middle of the 19th century when the dhimmis were enfranchised. The dhimmis were protected people, mostly Jews and Christians, who were protected by Muslim rulers as long as they paid extra taxes and agreed to be treated as second-class citizens. Due to a great amount of Western pressure, they were freed of this burden. Fundamentalist movement, however, have begun to erode this freedom.

There is also a smaller movement of Islamic extremism that is a political ideology that has come out of Fundamentalist Islam. Sometimes this extremism takes on the form of terrorism or warfare. Other Muslims contest the validity of these actions.

 # *Modern Traditions*

There are still traditions in modern Islam that are practiced in a similar way to early Muslims. Today Muslims still put a heavy focus on the Five Pillars of Islam. They also have a strong focus on worship in that they still practice a submission to God, confession of faith, and pray together.

It is common for Muslims to pronounce God's name before eating and drinking in order to recognize God's blessings on us. They also eat and drink with their right hand to remember that on the Day of Judgment Allah will get their records from right hands.

There is also the tradition of reciting the Adhaan in the right ear of newborn, which is a call to the complete submission to God's will, followed by the Iqaamah in its left ear, which is a call to be prepared to serve God. It is also important in Muslim tradition that they keep their nose, mouth, and teeth clean as well as washing after urination or defecation. The tradition of cleanliness is also perpetuated in the bathing after menstruation and sexual intercourse.

The two major annual festivals of Eid al-Adaa and Eid al-Fitr are also important Muslim traditions. Eid al-Fitr is celebrated at the end of Ramadhan, which is the month of fasting. Eid al-Adaa is celebrated on the 10th of Dhulhajj, which is the last month of the year when Muslims make their pilgrimage to Mecca.

© 2012 Breely Crush Publishing, LLC

Nature of God

To a Muslim, God is "One," and the monotheism is absolute. There is no room for pluralism. The Arabic term for God is "Allah." Even Christian and Jewish Arabs use the term "Allah" for God. God is omnipotent and omniscient. They believe that Allah is the same God Abraham worshipped. Any attempt to create a visual image of God is discouraged, as it may promote idolatry. Plus, they believe that Allah is incorporeal, so it would be impossible to create a depiction.

Qur'an

The Qur'an is believed to be the final Word of God given to the prophet Muhammad via God's Angel Gabriel. In English it is often spelled out as Koran. Since the Muslims believe that Judaism and Christianity distorted the Word of God by altering the Hebrew Bible and adding the New Testament respectively, they believe this word sets it right. To Muslims the Qur'an is unchangeable and flawless.

The Qur'an was written sometime between 650 and 656, and Muslims believe that the Qur'an they read today is the same text. There is great veneration for the Qur'an. Muslims take great care with the written word often wrapping it in clean cloth, keeping the writing on a high shelf, and even washing prior to any readings and prayer. Old Qur'ans must be buried in soil, not thrown away.

Most Muslims will memorize portions of the Qur'an in its original language. However, it is thought that millions of people have memorized the entire book. These people are called hafiz.

Five Pillars of Islam

In Sunni Islam there are five fundamental tenets known as the Five Pillars of Islam. The Shi'a Muslims also have these five tenets, but they are known as the Roots of Religion. Shi'a Islam goes on to add ten other core practices, the Branches of Religion. The Five Pillars of Islam are:

Shahadah
Shahadah is testimony that states there is no other God worthy of worship than Allah and that Muhammad is His messenger.

Salat
Salat is the daily performance of five prayers. One must face Mecca when performing these prayers.

Sawm
Sawm is performed during Ramadan, and it is a fast that lasts from dawn to dusk.

Zakat/Zahaah
Zakat is the act of giving alms.

Hajj
During the month of Dhu al-Hijjah occurs the Pilgrimage to Mecca. It is mandatory that a Muslim make this pilgrimage to Mecca at least once in a lifetime as long as the person has the ability to do so.

Shari'ah

Shari'ah is Islamic law, and its main source is the Qur'an. In the early Muslim community the Sunnah of Muhammad was also used. The Shari'ah contains laws that refer to all aspects of life including foreign relations and daily living.

Hudud laws are those specific to the Qur'an. They refer to the crimes of theft, highway robbery, intoxications, adultery, and falsely accusing another of adultery. The punishment for these crimes cannot be mitigated.

There are also laws relating to inheritance, money, prayer, charity, fasting, and more. The Qur'an's laws are rather broad, so the practice is more varied. The Ulema, or scholars, created elaborate legal systems based on those rules and the Sunnah. If one does not understand the Arabic Qur'an, then a mufti, or judge, will advise him or her.

Jihad

Jihad is a term meaning holy war. In some cases it is meant as the inward struggle for perfect faith, however today it is mostly associated with the military action used to further spread the Islamic nation. To Muslim scholars there are five types of jihad:

Jihad of the Heart/Soul
This type of jihad involves the struggle between good and evil for control of the mind.

                         © 2012 Breely Crush Publishing, LLC

Jihad by the Tongue
This type of jihad is the struggle between good and evil for speech and writing.

Jihad by the Pen and Knowledge
This is a struggle for good and evil through studying Islam, ijtihad, and sciences.

Jihad by the Hand
This type of jihad involves the struggle of good and evil in relation to a person's wealth. This would involve tasks such as going on the Hajj, taking care of elderly parents, furthering the cause of Islam, or even espionage.

Jihad by the Sword
This type of jihad is what many people in the West consider jihad, for it is the actual armed fighting of a holy war.

 # Wahhabi

The Wahhabi movement was an Islamic reform movement. Its purpose was a type of purification of Islam through returning to Muhammad and the Quran. It rejected all modifications that had been made to the Medina community just after Muhammad's death. The movement was named for its founder Muhammad ibn Abd al-Wahhab. The movement urged simplicity, without wine or tobacco, and forbid music and gold ornaments. Unitarianism was strongly emphasized. When the Wahhabis captured Mecca in 1806 they destroyed the tombs where the pilgrims worshipped, believing it to be a form of polytheistic worship.

 # Saladin

Saladin was the best known Muslim warrior of the 12th century. He became a leader at the time of the crusades. He seized power for the Sunnites in Egypt, and then went on to recapture Jerusalem in 1187. After continued fighting he eventually made a truce in 1192 which gave the interior to Muslims and the coast to Christians. It also allowed Christian pilgrims to enter Jerusalem.

Sikhism

Sikhism developed from a merging, in a way, of Muslim and Hindu. While it is a doctrine all its own, it has many of the basic beliefs of the two. The founder of Sikhism is Nanak. One day after bathing in the river, Nanak disappeared for three days during which he had a vision from God (or The True Name). It was after this that he set about preaching. He spent years wandering India, singing and preaching in marketplaces, open squares, and street corners. However, it wasn't until he reached Punjab that he had any success. It was there that a group of disciples, or Sikhs, formed.

    © 2012 Breely Crush Publishing, LLC

Sample Test Questions

1) This religious orientation desires a union with a reality greater than oneself.

    A) Mystical
    B) Communal
    C) Prophetic
    D) Apocalyptic

The correct answer is A:) Mystical.

2) Sikhs and Hindus share which belief system?

    A) Polytheism
    B) Living gurus
    C) Reincarnation
    D) Caste systems

The correct answer is C:) Reincarnation.

3) During the Roman Empire, which community of Jews fled to the wilderness due to apocalyptic visions?

    A) Christians
    B) Sadducees
    C) Essenes
    D) Zealots

The correct answer is C:) Essenes.

4) In the 19th Century, which movement believed that the source of understanding came from emotion or intuition rather than reason?

    A) Enlightenment
    B) Romanticism
    C) Judaism
    D) Revivalism

The correct answer is B:) Romanticism.

5) The Tanakh is an acronym for what division of the Hebrew Bible?

   A) The first five books
   B) The epistles
   C) The Pentateuch
   D) The three major divisions

The correct answer is D:) The three major divisions.

6) What does "Shinto" mean?

   A) The Land of the Gods
   B) Ancestral way persons
   C) The Way of the Gods
   D) Protectors of Buddha's Law

The correct answer is C:) The Way of the Gods. Part of the Shinto myth is that Japan was once peopled exclusively with kami, or deities.

7) The feminine aspect of the divine is celebrated in which alternative religion?

   A) Baha'i
   B) Hare Krishna
   C) Wicca
   D) Druidism

The correct answer is C:) Wicca.

8) Which of these is the oldest school of Tibetan Buddhism?

   A) Nyingma-pa
   B) Tzen-tsu
   C) Kagyu-pa
   D) T'ien-ming

The correct answer is A:) Nyingma-pa.

    © 2012 Breely Crush Publishing, LLC

9) According to Hinduism, which describes a sannayasin?

A) A person who has disavowed any worldly goods in order to life a life of asceticism and seek moksha.
B) The person who uses the Ayurvedic technique to heal illnesses and preserve life.
C) A person who has achieved a oneness of the mind and senses and abandoned all states of existence through Yoga.
D) The person who finds a balance between worldly pleasures and spiritual desires.

The correct answer is A:) A person who has disavowed any worldly goods in order to life a life of asceticism and seek moksha.

10) The Imam Mahdi are to the Shiites as _____ is to Christians.

A) Mary's virgin birth
B) Christ's divinity
C) The Holy Ghost
D) Christ's Second Coming

The correct answer is D:) Christ's Second Coming.

11) How many books of scripture does the Mormon Church believe in?

A) 5
B) 4
C) 3
D) 2

The correct answer is A:) 5. They are the Old Testament, New Testament, Book of Mormon, Doctrine and Covenants, and Pearl of Great Price.

12) The founder of Zen Buddhism was an Indian Monk named Bodhidharma. In which century was the Zen school of thought founded?

A) 5th century AD
B) 3rd century AD
C) 6th century AD
D) 4th century AD

The correct answer is C:) 6th century AD.

13) Jains believe the highest stage of life, short of liberation is

    A) Birth as a human
    B) Birth as a fish
    C) Becoming a parent
    D) Getting married

The correct answer is A:) Birth as a human.

14) In which continent can primal religions be found?

    A) Australia
    B) North America
    C) South America
    D) All of the above

The correct answer is D:) All of the above.

15) What was Paul of Tarsus' originally intending to do when he reached Damascus?

    A) Worship at the Temple
    B) Arrest members of the Christ-worshipping church
    C) Convert people to Christianity
    D) Receive communion

The correct answer is B:) Arrest members of the Christ-worshipping church.

16) Which value is not Taoist?

    A) Formal education
    B) Simplicity
    C) Spontaneity
    D) Appreciation of nature's movements

The correct answer is A:) Formal education.

17) Where did the monastic movement in Christianity begin?

    A) Spain
    B) Russia
    C) Rome
    D) Egypt

The correct answer is D:) Egypt.

 © 2012 Breely Crush Publishing, LLC

18) Where is the Mahayana Buddhism strongest today?

    A) India
    B) Japan
    C) China
    D) Spain

The correct answer is B:) Japan.

19) The Hindu yogic path that most emphasizes rational thought as the way to liberation is

    A) Bhakti
    B) Karma
    C) Jnana
    D) Rana

The correct answer is C:) Jnana.

20) Which of the following is NOT true of a get?

    A) A man must present his wife with a get to be considered divorced.
    B) The wife is no longer considered a married woman and the laws of adultery no longer apply.
    C) The wife is returned the legal rights which the husband held in marriage.
    D) All of the above are true.

The correct answer is D:) All of the above are true. Answers A, B, and C are all correct statements.

21) What term describes a religion that worships one God but accepts that other religions have other deities?

    A) Polytheistic
    B) Ecumenical
    C) Henothiest
    D) Philosophist

The correct answer is C:) Henothiest.

22) The Rig Veda contains hymns that

    A) Lay out the specific doctrines and beliefs of the Vedic religion
    B) Tell believers how to perform sacrificial rituals
    C) Are sung along with rituals as melodies and chants
    D) Offer praise to the Gods to ask them for things like wealth, long life, and victory

The correct answer is D:) Offer praise to the Gods to ask them for things like wealth, long life, and victory.

23) Who started the Reconstructionalist sect?

    A) Abraham Geiger
    B) Rabbi Mordecai Kaplan
    C) Moses Mendelssohn
    D) None of the above

The correct answer is B:) Rabbi Mordecai Kaplan. It was developed as a modernized form of Judaism.

24) The mystic teachings of the sacrificial Hindu religion are called the

    A) Aranyakas
    B) Puranas
    C) Brahmanas
    D) Upanishads

The correct answer is A:) Aranyakas.

25) Which of the following is NOT considered by the Mormon Church to be a book of scripture?

    A) The Book of Mormon
    B) Doctrine and Covenants
    C) The Pearl of Great Price
    D) All of the above are considered scripture

The correct answer is D:) All of the above are considered scripture.

© 2012 Breely Crush Publishing, LLC

26) According to the Jain, which being is not one-sensed?

A) Earth
B) Water
C) Insects
D) Vegetation

The correct answer is C:) Insects.

27) During which holiday does Islam require fasting?

A) Al-Hijira
B) Ramadan
C) Hajj
D) Aid al-Haddah

The correct answer is B:) Ramadan.

28) Approximately how many Jews are in Spain today?

A) 100
B) 1,200
C) 12,000
D) 150,000

The correct answer is C:) 12,000.

29) What factor was most significant in the division of the kingdom of Israel into the nations of Israel and Judah in 928 AD?

A) The Assyrian invasion
B) Disagreements over the meaning of certain scripture
C) Rehoboam's implementation of high taxes
D) The practice of idolatry in the Southern kingdom

The correct answer is C:) Rehoboam's implementation of high taxes.

30) Which is the most likely symbol of the female divinity in primal religions?

    A) Water and spears
    B) Clouds and moon
    C) Trees and rocks
    D) Spirals and eggs

The correct answer is D:) Spirals and eggs.

31) What is the name for the Jewish holiday which is celebrated as the Day of Atonement?

    A) Yom Kippur
    B) Lag BaOmer
    C) Tzom Gedalia
    D) Rosh Hashanah

The correct answer is A:) Yom Kippur.

32) Which movement, started in the 1960's, brought Pentecostal elements like speaking in tongues to mainstream Protestant churches and the Roman Catholic Church?

    A) Evangelical
    B) Charismatic
    C) Ecumenical
    D) Revivalist

The correct answer is B:) Charismatic.

33) What is the name of Jews that maintain their Judaism but also belief in Jesus Christ as Lord and Savior?

    A) Messianic Jews
    B) Hassidic Jews
    C) Orthodox Jews
    D) Mitzvah Jews

The correct answer is A:) Messianic Jews.

© 2012 Breely Crush Publishing, LLC

34) Which of the five relationships in Confucianism characterizes "filial piety"?

A) Ruler to Ruled
B) Father to Son
C) Husband to Wife
D) Friend to Friend

The correct answer is B:) Father to Son

35) The rigid caste system outlined in Hinduism is called

A) Vendu
B) Haddassah
C) Brahma
D) Shudra

The correct answer is A:) Vendu.

36) How old was Muhammad when he had his vision of the Angel Gabriel?

A) 10
B) 20
C) 40
D) 80

The correct answer is C:) 40. Although he began questioning early than 40, it was when he was about 40 that Muhammad received his vision and began thinking of himself as a prophet.

37) This type of Confucianism is laden with Buddhist and Taoist concepts

A) Neo-Confucianism
B) I-Ching Confucianism
C) Han Confucianism
D) Jen Confucianism

The correct answer is A:) Neo-Confucianism.

38) Which day of the week is the Jewish Shabbat?

    A) Monday
    B) Friday
    C) Saturday
    D) Sunday

The correct answer is C:) Saturday.

39) The name for God in the Sikh religion is

    A) Abu Ghraib
    B) The True Name
    C) The One and Only
    D) Brahman

The correct answer is B:) The True Name.

40) Which of the following is a correct statement about the Ka'bah?

    A) All praying is directed toward the Ka'bah.
    B) No unclean activity should be done while facing the Ka'bah.
    C) Nothing is allowed to cross in the column of air above the Ka'bah.
    D) All of the above.

The correct answer is D:) All of the above. A, B, and C are all correct statements about the Ka'bah.

41) Which of these is not one of the Four Affirmations of Shinto?

    A) Physical cleanliness
    B) Tradition
    C) Worship
    D) Sacrificing of Self

The correct answer is D:) Sacrificing of Self.

© 2012 Breely Crush Publishing, LLC

42) In Christianity, the Nicene Creed strongly emphasizes

    A) The fulfillment of prophecies through Jesus
    B) Jesus' compassion for humanity
    C) Paul's journey
    D) Jesus' equality with God

The correct answer is D:) Jesus' equality with God.

43) Which caliph defended Islam against the crusaders?

    A) Saladin
    B) 'Uthman
    C) Umayyad
    D) Abu Hanifa

The correct answer is A:) Saladin.

44) When one practices Raja Yoga, he or she is trying to reach a state of _____ where the mind is totally under the person's control.

    A) Nirvana
    B) Moksha
    C) Samadhi
    D) Dharma

The correct answer is C:) Samadhi.

45) Which of the following does the Eastern Orthodox church believe in?

    A) Purgatory
    B) Papal Infallibility
    C) Baptism
    D) The Pope

The correct answer is C:) Baptism. Baptism is considered to be a way to cleanse oneself from sin.

46) Which of these groups was the most liberal thinking in Ancient China?

    A) Xunzi
    B) Taoists
    C) Reformers
    D) Confucians

The correct answer is B:) Taoists.

47) Which of these is one of six basic duties of the laity to the Jain?

    A) Renouncing certain foods
    B) Being indifferent to the body
    C) Showing respect for teachers
    D) All of the above

The correct answer is D:) All of the above.

48) Which approach to religion relates answers to a systematic whole through an adherence to reason instead of religious authority?

    A) Philosophy
    B) Sociology
    C) Mythology
    D) Mysticism

The correct answer is A:) Philosophy.

49) Which of the following is a true statement about the Catholic view of sacraments?

    A) All sacraments are necessary in every case for salvation.
    B) Sacraments are effective regardless of the receiver's disposition.
    C) The sacraments are not necessary.
    D) The sacraments build, nourish, and strengthen faith.

The correct answer is D:) The sacraments build, nourish, and strengthen faith. It is not required that every person receives every sacrament, however, in the general sense it is believed that the sacraments are necessary for salvation. Also, their effectiveness is influenced by disposition.

© 2012 Breely Crush Publishing, LLC

50) Christians use this term that refers to the Second coming of Jesus Christ

    A) Messiah
    B) Revelation
    C) Rapture
    D) Liturgy

The correct answer is C:) Rapture.

51) This is the name for the texts that provides the Jews with the ritual and tradition that can be enforced in Jewish courts

    A) Nevi'im
    B) Menorah
    C) Gamarah
    D) Halakah

The correct answer is D:) Halakah.

52) What town was Jesus from?

    A) Bethlehem
    B) Jerusalem
    C) Nazareth
    D) None of the above

The correct answer is C:) Nazareth. While he was born in Bethlehem and died in Jerusalem, Christ grew up in Nazareth.

53) A person can recognize a Theravada Buddhist monk by the fact that he

    A) Wears an orange robe
    B) Does not eat meat
    C) Adorns his head with jewels
    D) Practices elaborate daily rituals

The correct answer is A:) Wears an orange robe.

54) Which time period is considered the "Golden Age" of Islamic civilization?

    A) Muhammad returning to Mecca
    B) Ottoman Age
    C) Abassid Dynasty
    D) Umayyad Dynasty

The correct answer is C:) Abassid Dynasty.

55) Traditional Native American vision quests were performed to serve what purpose?

    A) To get in touch with the dead
    B) To predict the future
    C) To gain insight from the spirit world
    D) To read the thoughts of others

The correct answer is C:) To gain insight from the spirit world.

56) Which of the following did Ulrich Zwingli NOT believe?

    A) Worship needed to return to the doctrine of the Old Testament.
    B) The Sacrament should be taken symbolically.
    C) Ritual should be kept at a minimum.
    D) Worship should not include anything which is not commanded.

The correct answer is A:) Worship needed to return to the doctrine of the Old Testament. Zwingli was an advocate for the New Testament.

57) The Dogon Tribe of West Africa use rites and sacrifices in order to

    A) Distinguish men from women
    B) Bring rain and thunder
    C) Praise Gods
    D) Restore order

The correct answer is D:) Restore order.

 © 2012 Breely Crush Publishing, LLC

58) Where was Ulrich Zwingli from?

    A) Germany
    B) Switzerland
    C) France
    D) England

The correct answer is B:) Switzerland.

59) Muslims perform the annual pilgrimage to Mecca, or Hajj, in order to commemorate

    A) Muhammad's victory over Mecca when he returned from Medina
    B) Aspects of Abraham's life
    C) Muhammad's revelation from the Angel Gabriel
    D) Almsgiving

The correct answer is B:) Aspects of Abraham's life.

60) Jews traditionally hang this item in a doorway which contains a scroll of parchment containing the opening lines of the shema in order to remember their religious obligation to God.

    A) Tephllin
    B) Tallit
    C) Kippah
    D) Mezuzah

The correct answer is D:) Mezuzah.

61) Who is considered the first Christian martyr?

    A) Jesus Christ
    B) Stephen
    C) Peter
    D) Paul

The correct answer is B:) Stephen. Stephen was stoned for preaching about Christ.

62) Which of these is not the name of a main type of Shinto shrine

    A) Shrines of local significance that house the kami of the locality
    B) Inari Shrines
    C) Izumo Shrines
    D) Haiden

The correct answer is D:) Haiden.

63) This is the name of the Japanese sect that is mystically inclined, placing an emphasis on meditation.

    A) Shingon Sect
    B) Tandai Sect
    C) Amida Sects
    D) None of the above

The correct answer is A:) Shingon Sect.

64) Why is Paul considered one of the most notable leaders of the early church?

    A) Because it is widely known that Jesus thought he was the best apostle.
    B) He wrote the Pauline Epistles which comprise 13 books in the New Testament.
    C) He had the most interesting conversion story and kept detailed records.
    D) The people found him easier to listen to then most of the other apostles.

The correct answer is B:) He wrote the Pauline Epistles which comprise 13 books in the New Testament.

65) In Hinduism, this is the ten-day celebration given in honor of Kali.

    A) Holi
    B) Ramadhan
    C) Dasara
    D) Divali

The correct answer is C:) Dasara.

 © 2012 Breely Crush Publishing, LLC

66) In the Balbua Tribe, a person's name represents

    A) His date of birth
    B) His nature
    C) His profession
    D) All of the above

The correct answer is B:) His nature.

67) Which of the following is NOT a Catholic sacrament?

    A) Birth
    B) Baptism
    C) Anointing of the sick
    D) Holy Orders

The correct answer is A:) Birth. Baptism, Anointing of the sick and Holy Orders are all Catholic sacraments.

68) This group included followers of a variety of religious movements in early Christianity that put an emphasis on salvation through secret knowledge.

    A) Gnostics
    B) Hassids
    C) Pentecostals
    D) Reformers

The correct answer is A:) Gnostics.

69) Which of these individuals in not considered one of the Five Major Prophets by Islam?

    A) Moses
    B) Jesus
    C) Abraham
    D) David

The correct answer is D:) David.

© 2012 Breely Crush Publishing, LLC

70) Who is the leader of the Shiites?

A) Imam
B) Abu Bakr
C) 'Umar
D) 'Uthman

The correct answer is A:) Imam. Abu Bakr, 'Umar, and 'Uthman are the three caliphs which are not believed in by the Shiites. They even curse them in their Friday prayers.

71) Confucius described Heaven as being

A) A supernatural kingdom where the souls of ancestors resided
B) The reason for all the change in the world
C) Where the recently departed souls would wait for judgment
D) A higher power and law that expelled the patterns of former Gods

The correct answer is D:) A higher power and law that expelled the patterns of former Gods.

72) Which of the following would NOT be a typical belief of a Sadducee?

A) The Books of Moses should be interpreted literally.
B) Religious unrest is a dangerous occurrence, to be frowned upon.
C) Cultural innovation which improves relationships abroad should be welcomed.
D) All of the above statements would be typical views of a Sadducee.

The correct answer is D:) All of the above statements would be typical views of a Sadducee. The Sadducees were both political and religious leaders. Therefore, their efforts were concentrated on keeping economic and religious stability.

73) This philosophical argument believes that the proof of God's existence is implied in the idea of God itself is known as

A) Theological
B) Historical
C) Ontological
D) Cosmological

The correct answer is C:) Ontological.

© 2012 Breely Crush Publishing, LLC

74) Which of the following is NOT a Jewish Holiday?

    A) Yom Kippur
    B) Lag BaOmer
    C) Yom Pesach
    D) Tzom Gedalia

The correct answer is C:) Yom Pesach. While Pesach is a holiday, Yom Pesach is not.

75) It is believed that Confucianism probably grew out of _____ of the time.

    A) Concern for the economy
    B) Sociological concerns
    C) Concern over education
    D) Philosophical concerns

The correct answer is B:) Sociological concerns.

76) In the 20th century a movement began to try and unite the different factions of Christianity. What is it called?

    A) Ecumenism
    B) Unitarianism
    C) Hedonism
    D) Catechism

The correct answer is A:) Ecumenism.

77) Which of the following is NOT true of Zealots?

    A) The movement is considered to have first started around 6 AD.
    B) They believed that submission to Roman rule was forsaking God.
    C) They were considered by the Romans to be bandits and robbers.
    D) After being viciously suppressed, the Zealot movement died out.

The correct answer is D:) After being viciously suppressed, the Zealot movement died out. Even after their first revolution came to a bloody end, the Zealot's held to their beliefs.

© 2012 Breely Crush Publishing, LLC

78) What are Jews in Spain called?

  A) Sephardi Jews
  B) Shekina Jews
  C) Amoraim Jews
  D) None of the above

The correct answer is A:) Sephardi Jews. Sephardi is essentially translated as Spain.

79) In Taoism, there is a social ideal that is revealed in what work?

  A) I Ching
  B) Tao-Te Ching
  C) Five Pillars
  D) Classic of Great Peace

The correct answer is D:) Classic of Great Peace.

80) What is the name of the rock that Muslim's take pilgrimages to see?

  A) Ka'bah
  B) Quyrash
  C) Hajj
  D) Habak

The correct answer is A:) Ka'bah. People circle it seven times and kiss it in hopes of receiving heaven's blessing.

81) Which of these things does NOT need to be present to make a Hindu marriage legal?

  A) A gift by the father on behalf of the bride
  B) The bride and groom taking seven steps around the fire
  C) The bride and groom seated on a platform
  D) The holding of hands

The correct answer is C:) The bride and groom seated on a platform.

© 2012 Breely Crush Publishing, LLC

82) When did the Jewish Diaspora begin?

    A) 12th century BC
    B) 8th century BC
    C) 1st century AD
    D) 1948

The correct answer is B:) 8th century BC. This is considered to be the beginning of the Diaspora because it is when the ancient states of Israel and Judah were conquered.

83) In Judaism, the Bar Mitzvah is celebrated to signify the coming of age of the male. What is the celebration for the female?

    A) Bat Mitzvah
    B) Bah Mitzvah
    C) Bah'ai Mitzvah
    D) All of the above

The correct answer is A:) Bat Mitzvah. Bat Mitzvah is the name of the event for girls and Bar Mitzvah is the name for boys.

84) Who enslaved the Jews in Egypt?

    A) Moses
    B) God
    C) Pharaoh
    D) None of the above

The correct answer is C:) Pharaoh.

85) This belief states that human action and all other events are caused by something outside of the human will.

    A) Structuralism
    B) Humanism
    C) Animism
    D) Determinism

The correct answer is D:) Determinism.

© 2012 Breely Crush Publishing, LLC

86) What is considered the birth of Islam?

    A) The migration from Mecca to Medina
    B) The day Muhammad was born
    C) When Muhammad first began teaching the people of Mecca
    D) When Muhammad received his first revelation

The correct answer is A:) The migration from Mecca to Medina. When Muhammad was forced to flee Mecca on a camel, he miraculously made the eleven day journey to Medina in nine days.

87) In traditional Chinese religion, the reason an emperor ruled over the land was because

    A) God came down and lived within the emperor
    B) He had vanquished those who opposed him
    C) He was virtuous and received the Mandate of Heaven
    D) It was his right from birth

The correct answer is C:) He was virtuous and received the Mandate of Heaven.

88) What does the Jewish Diaspora mean today?

    A) It is the term for Jewish people living outside the State of Israel.
    B) It is the term for the displacement of Jewish people in the 8th century.
    C) Diaspora is a holiday celebrated by Jewish people.
    D) None of the above

The correct answer is A:) It is a term for Jewish people living outside the State of Israel. While historically the term describes Jewish people forced to leave Israel, it now refers to people living outside Israel.

89) Tantras are most closely associated with which branch of Buddhism?

    A) Theravada
    B) Mahayana
    C) Vajrayana
    D) None of the above

The correct answer is C:) Vajrayana.

 © 2012 Breely Crush Publishing, LLC

90) What sect of Judaism is most prevalent?

    A) Haredi
    B) Hiloni
    C) Masorti
    D) None of the above

The correct answer is B:) Hiloni. More than half of all Jewish people identify themselves as Hiloni, or secular.

91) During what time period was the Reconstructionalist sect developed?

    A) Prior to 1700
    B) 1860's-1890's
    C) 1920's-1940's
    D) After 1950

The correct answer is C:) 1920's-1940's. During this time Rabbi Mordecai Kaplan developed the Reconstructionalist sect.

92) Who specifically was Muhammad fleeing from?

    A) Yathrib
    B) Quyrash
    C) Medina
    D) Abu Bakr

The correct answer is B:) Quyrash. The Quyrash determined to strike when they heard of Muhammad's plan to migrate to Medina and establish himself there.

93) Which Judaic tribe is most likely the biggest contributor to the Rabbinic tradition?

    A) Pharisees
    B) Nazarites
    C) Maccabees
    D) Sadducees

The correct answer is A:) Pharisees.

94) The Unification Church got its nickname, The Moonies, from

  A) Their worship of the moon
  B) A prejudice of Judaic Theologists
  C) Their founder, Sun Myung Moon
  D) All of the above

The correct answer is C:) Their founder, Sun Myung Moon.

95) How long did the Jews wander in the desert before entering the Promised Land?

  A) 1 year
  B) 10 years
  C) 20 years
  D) 40 years

The correct answer is D:) 40 years. The people feared to attack the current inhabitants of the land and were forced to wander for 40 years before entering the Promised Land.

96) Which of the following is NOT a translation of Yahweh?

  A) I will be what I want to be
  B) I am that I am
  C) I am he that causes to be
  D) All of the above

The correct answer is D:) All of the above. Answers A, B, and C are all translations of Yahweh.

97) What is the word for a divorce granted by a rabbi?

  A) Get
  B) Lo tov
  C) Beit knesset
  D) None of the above

The correct answer is A:) Get.

                    © 2012 Breely Crush Publishing, LLC

98) Which of the following is NOT an aspect of Postmodernism?

    A) Our culture molds us to think in certain ways
    B) You construct your own reality
    C) Nothing can actually be proven
    D) People can judge other cultures and religions as wrong

The correct answer is D:) People can judge other cultures and religions as wrong.

99) What is Bar Mitzvah translated as?

    A) Son of righteousness
    B) Keeper of the commandments
    C) Son of the commandments
    D) None of the above

The correct answer is C:) Son of the commandments. It is the name not only of the ceremony, but the term for the 13 year old boy.

100) Hare Krishna believe that chanting the name of Krishna over and over is the only way to achieve freedom from

    A) Sanskrit
    B) Samsara
    C) Vishnu
    D) Brahma

The correct answer is B:) Samsara.

101) Which of the following is NOT true?

    A) Muhammad believed in the doctrine of final judgment and punishment of the wicked.
    B) Although he never read the Bible, Muhammad accepted Christianity and Judaism as parallel religions.
    C) The Allah of Islam is the same God as is accepted by Jewish and Christian religions.
    D) All of the above are true.

The correct answer is B:) Although he never read the Bible, Muhammad accepted Christianity and Judaism as parallel religions. In fact, Muhammad had an understanding of both the Old and New Testaments. He used that information to help him understand his own revelations.

102) According to the Chuang-tzu, the Tao is

    A) Complete
    B) All-embracing
    C) The One
    D) All of the above

The correct answer is D:) All of the above.

103) What was the name of the son that Abraham was commanded to sacrifice?

    A) Jacob
    B) Abraham
    C) Isaac
    D) None of the above

The correct answer is C:) Isaac. Abraham was commanded to sacrifice Isaac as a test of his faith, but was allowed to sacrifice a ram instead.

104) Which of the following is the name for the day when the Jewish people mourn the destruction of the temple in 70 AD?

    A) Tishah B'av
    B) Shavuot
    C) Pesach
    D) Purim

The correct answer is A:) Tishah B'av.

105) The Mishnah and Germara are the two major components of what book?

    A) Talmud
    B) Torah
    C) Bible
    D) None of the above

The correct answer is A:) Talmud. This book is second only to the Hebrew Bible in Judaism.

 © 2012 Breely Crush Publishing, LLC

106) This is the name of the Greek God who protected travelers and brought good luck. He is often portrayed as a messenger.

    A) Hermes
    B) Zeus
    C) Aphrodite
    D) Hercules

The correct answer is A:) Hermes.

107) What makes Hebrew a complex language?

    A) The letters of the alphabet also stand for numbers.
    B) There are thousands of letters, but no numbers.
    C) There are ambiguous meanings to almost all the words.
    D) Hebrew is a fairly simple language.

The correct answer is A:) The letters of the alphabet also stand for numbers. Numbers also have symbolisms of their own, allowing for many interpretations of the language.

108) The early Mayan Gods had a dual character, which types of duality existed in their Gods?

    A) Benevolent and malevolent
    B) Male and female
    C) None of the above
    D) All of the above

The correct answer is D:) All of the above.

109) Which of these animals were considered sacred in Ancient Egypt, so they were commonly mummified and placed in with the dead?

    A) Bears
    B) Cats
    C) Crocodiles
    D) Baboons

The correct answer is B:) Cats.

110) What is the basic idea of Zionism?

    A) Jewish people are stronger than other nations and should be able to control them.
    B) The Jewish people should create secure areas in the neighborhoods where they live.
    C) The only way for the Jewish people to gain security is through creating a national home in Palestine.
    D) None of the above

The correct answer is C:) The only way for the Jewish people to gain security is through creating a national home in Palestine. This idea developed due to the extreme anti-Semitism of the 19th century.

111) The Bontocs of North Luzon place an emphasis on the movements of animals along with natural phenomena which are considered

    A) Tradition
    B) Omens
    C) Natural
    D) Taboo

The correct answer is B:) Omens.

112) What is the Mishnah?

    A) A component of the Talmud.
    B) A word meaning "repetition" in Hebrew.
    C) A large work containing references to legal decisions of rabbis in the past.
    D) All of the above.

The correct answer is D:) All of the above. The Mishnah is one of the two major parts of the Talmud, or the book of laws.

113) In Confucianism, a man is considered ideal if he

    A) Was free from material desires
    B) Was born to nobility
    C) Found enlightenment
    D) Earned honor through personal effort

The correct answer is D:) Earned honor through personal effort.

 © 2012 Breely Crush Publishing, LLC

114) Who did Muhammad see in vision?

    A) Allah
    B) Angel Gabriel
    C) Zainab
    D) None of the above

The correct answer is B:) Angel Gabriel

115) The Hindu believe that Rama is one of the ten avatars of

    A) Dharma
    B) Vedas
    C) Vishnu
    D) Sita

The correct answer is C:) Vishnu.

116) Which of the following terms do NOT relate to the Upanishads?

    A) Rig Veda
    B) Bhagavad Gita
    C) Karma Yoga
    D) All of the above relate to the Upanishads

The correct answer is D:) All of the above relate to the Upanishads. Answers A, B, and C all relate to the Upanishads.

117) This item is often the focal point of a procession in a Shinto festival

    A) Kami
    B) Gion
    C) Mikoshi
    D) Sake

The correct answer is C:) Mikoshi.

118) What was the first sect to embrace Zionism?

   A) Tradition
   B) Orthodox
   C) Reconstructionalist
   D) All embraced it equally

The correct answer is B:) Orthodox. The Orthodox Jews were the first to embrace Zionism.

119) Why did Muhammad accept Christian and Judaism as parallel religions?

   A) He accepted the idea of final judgment and punishment of the wicked, which are supported by both Christians and Jews.
   B) He read the Old and New Testament
   C) Allah who he received the revelation from is the same God that the Jews and Christians believed in.
   D) All of the above.

The correct answer is D:) All of the above.

120) Which of the following is one of the four sources of the sacred law of Islam, or Shari'a?

   A) Sunna
   B) Ijma
   C) Qiyas
   D) All of the above

The correct answer is D:) All of the above.

121) Which of the following is true of Chuang Tzu?

   A) He was an influential Chinese philosopher.
   B) He turned Lao Tzu philosophies from mystical to transcendental.
   C) He believed life was continually changing.
   D) All of the above

The correct answer is D:) All of the above. Answers A, B, and C are all true statements about Chuang Tzu.

122) In Christianity, Pentecost is a festival to celebrate

    A) The day when God sent the Holy Spirit to the Apostles marking the birth of the church.
    B) The resurrection and ascension of Jesus to Heaven.
    C) The solemnity of the passion of Jesus.
    D) The forty days Jesus spent fasting in the wilderness, and his victory over Satan.

The correct answer is A:) The day when God sent the Holy Spirit to the Apostles marking the birth of the church.

123) What is the newest form of Buddhism?

    A) Theravada
    B) Mahayana
    C) Vajrayana
    D) None of the above

The correct answer is B:) Mahayana. Of the two branches, Mahayana and Theravada, Mahayana is the newest.

124) What is the name for the being which seek "Buddahood" to benefit all sentient beings?

    A) Bodhistattva
    B) Theravadin
    C) Magadha
    D) Mandalas

The correct answer is A:) Bodhistattva. These beings seek perfection for the benefit of all sentient beings. Therefore since Buddha is perfect, they seek "Buddahood."

125) Which of the following is NOT a belief of Zoroastrianism?

    A) Final victory of Ahura Mazda
    B) There are many deities besides Ahura Mazda
    C) Judgment of individual souls
    D) Modes of Good Action

The correct answer is B:) There are many deities outside Ahura Mazda. Zoroaster's teachings were strictly monotheistic (belief in one God).

126) Which of these terms is not used as a name for Confucianism?

    A) Ju
    B) Hsun-tzu
    C) Ju-chiao
    D) K'ung-chiao

The correct answer is B:) Hsun-tzu.

127) To which religion was Emperor Asoka converted?

    A) Hindu
    B) Buddhism
    C) Sikhism
    D) Taoism

The correct answer is B:) Buddhism. The emperor felt guilty due to the suffering of the people so he converted to and helped spread Buddhism.

128) Where is St. Paul from?

    A) Jerusalem
    B) Damascus
    C) Bethlehem
    D) Tarsus

The correct answer is D:) Tarsus. St. Paul is also known as Paul of Tarsus.

129) Which of the following is NOT true of Sikhism?

    A) Sikhism is an equal mix of Muslim and Hindu, with no uniqueness to it.
    B) Nanak received a vision from God after which he began to preach.
    C) Nanak didn't have much success until he reached Punjab.
    D) All of the above are true

The correct answer is A:) Sikhism is an equal mix of Muslim and Hindu, with no uniqueness to it. While Sikhism developed from a merging, in a way, of Muslim and Hindu, and has many of the basic beliefs of the two, it is a unique doctrine.

© 2012 Breely Crush Publishing, LLC

130) Which are some of the basic differences between primal religions and the Judaic-based belief systems?

A) Primal religions are polytheistic and Judaic religions are monotheistic
B) Primal religions mix magic and religion while Judaic religions do not
C) Primal religions put an emphasis on sacrifice and ritual while Judaic systems put more emphasis on worship
D) All of the above

The correct answer is D:) All of the above.

131) Which two countries have a higher Shiite population than Sunni population?

A) Iran and India
B) India and Iraq
C) Iran and Iraq
D) Iraq and Pakistan

The correct answer is C:) Iran and Iraq. About 50% of all Shiites live in either Iran or Iraq.

132) In Hinduism, dharma means

A) The ideas presented in the Bhagavad-Gita
B) A set of inalienable truths
C) The ongoing cycle of rebirths
D) Religion and social duty

The correct answer is D:) Religion and social duty.

133) Which of the following would be a typical belief of a Sadducee?

A) Religious innovation allows for expression of opinion, and is important.
B) The Sadducees have the most reasonable view of the world and how things should work.
C) Cultural innovations are dangerous and should be frowned upon.
D) All of the above statements would be typical views of a Sadducee.

The correct answer is B:) The Sadducees have the most reasonable view of the world and how things should work. However, while the Sadducees considered themselves more reasonable, many of the people thought their opinions to be clouded by their many roles.

134) Who is the founder of Sikhism?

    A) Angad
    B) Nanak
    C) Kartarpur
    D) Kabir

The correct answer is B:) Nanak. Nanak received a vision from God after which he began to preach.

135) Off the Sunni schools of thought today, which school has the most conservative doctrine?

    A) Safi'ite
    B) Shi'a
    C) Hanbalite
    D) Malkite

The correct answer is C:) Hanbalite.

136) Which two religions influenced Sikhism?

    A) Hindu and Muslim
    B) Hindu and Christianity
    C) Christianity and Muslim
    D) Muslim and Shinto

The correct answer is A:) Hindu and Muslim

137) Which of the following is NOT true of the Wahhabi movement?

    A) Its purpose was a return to strict adherence to Muhammad and the Quran.
    B) The movement was responsible for building tombs and shrines to holy men and women.
    C) Music, gold ornaments, wine and tobacco were all forbidden.
    D) It rejected all modifications which had been made to the Medina community.

The correct answer is B:) The movement was responsible for building tombs and shrines to holy men and women. Rather, the Wahhabis destroyed shrines and tombs in Mecca where the pilgrims came to pray. They considered it polytheistic, and therefore didn't believe in it.

138) Which of the following was allowed by Wahhabis?

    A) Music
    B) Wine
    C) Prayer
    D) Gold Ornamentation

The correct answer is C:) Prayer. Games such as chess were even forbidden because they might make people forget the hours of prayer.

139) The Adi Granth is the holy book for which religion?

    A) Sikhism
    B) Islam
    C) Eastern Orthodox
    D) Mormonism

The correct answer is A:) Sikhism. The Adi Granth was compiled by Arjan, fearing that the hymns would be lost. Most of them were written by either Arjan or Nanak.

140) Mencius addressed the concepts of good and evil by stating that

    A) People are basically good, but evil comes from the environment.
    B) People are basically evil.
    C) People are neither good nor evil, so family influence pushed them in one direction or the other.
    D) People need not be concerned with good nor evil.

The correct answer is A:) People are basically good, but evil comes from the environment.

141) Which of the following is attributed to Saladin?

    A) Founding the Hanifite school of thought.
    B) Spreading Islam to Western Europe.
    C) Forcing Egypt to convert to Shiism.
    D) The recapture of Jerusalem in 1187.

The correct answer is D:) The recapture of Jerusalem in 1187.

142) In Medieval times, this theologian was responsible for the cosmological argument that God existed.

    A) Hidegard
    B) Thomas Aquinas
    C) Thomas a Becket
    D) Pope Benedict I

The correct answer is B:) Thomas Aquinas.

143) Which two churches were separated through the Great Schism?

    A) Roman Catholic and Lutheran
    B) Eastern Orthodox and Shinto
    C) Eastern Orthodox and Roman Catholic
    D) Shinto and Lutheran

The correct answer is C:) Eastern Orthodox and Roman Catholic.

144) What God does Zoroastrianism believe in?

    A) Zoroaster
    B) Angra Mainyu
    C) Vohu Manah
    D) Ahura Mazda

The correct answer is D:) Ahura Mazda. Ahura Mazda means Wise Lord or Supreme Being. Believers of Zoroastrianism believe that Ahura Mazda appeared to Zoroaster in vision when he was thirty.

145) According to the Maoris of New Zealand, the names of the guardians who warned of danger and gave encouragement were

    A) Te Aomarama
    B) Te Po
    C) Kaitiaki
    D) Mana

The correct answer is C:) Kaitiaki.

© 2012 Breely Crush Publishing, LLC

146) How was Stephen killed?

   A) Crucifixion
   B) Long imprisonment
   C) Stoning
   D) None of the above

The correct answer is C:) Stoning. Stephen was stoned after he called the judges at his trial murderers of the Son of God. At this the angry crowd took him into the streets and stoned him.

147) Muhammad believed that the highest point of jihad is

   A) The Holy War to spread Islam across the world
   B) The struggle over one's wealth
   C) The striving for good by studying Islam and the sciences
   D) The striving of the soul for purification

The correct answer is D:) The striving of the soul for purification.

148) Why do many churches now worship on Sundays?

   A) It is the day of the week on which Jesus was born.
   B) It is the day of the week on which Jesus was resurrected.
   C) It is the day of the week on which Jesus was crucified.
   D) It is the day of the week on which Jesus laid in the tomb.

The correct answer is B:) It is the day of the week on which Jesus was resurrected.

149) Which is the central tenet of the Lutheran Church?

   A) The Eucharist
   B) Faith
   C) Liturgy
   D) Music

The correct answer is B:) Faith.

150) Which of the following did Emperor Asoka NOT do?

   A) Promise to bear all wrongs with meekness and patience
   B) Convert to Buddhism
   C) Encouraged the spread of Buddhism
   D) Continue to eat meat in small amounts

The correct answer is D:) Continue to eat meat in small amounts. Emperor Asoka abolished meat consumption in the palace after converting to Buddhism.

151) Which three criteria must a person meet in the only mandatory criteria for the person to become a viable candidate for the Taoist Clergy?

   A) Have family approval
   B) Not be married
   C) Be under 30
   D) Be male

The correct answer is D:) Be male.

152) Which of the following is NOT a correct statement about the differences between Eastern Orthodox and Roman Catholic beliefs?

   A) The Orthodox church does not believe in original sin and the Catholic church does.
   B) The Catholic church supports papal infallibility, while the Orthodox church does not.
   C) Orthodox priests can marry prior to ordination and Catholic bishops cannot.
   D) Icons are essential to Orthodox worship, and not in Catholic worship.

The correct answer is A:) The Orthodox church does not believe in original sin and the Catholic church does. Both churches believe in the concept of original sin, they just have different interpretations of its effects.

© 2012 Breely Crush Publishing, LLC

153) Abortion has become a common practice in Hindu society. What is the major reason for its prevalence?

    A) The desire for a certain sex of child
    B) The influence of Western culture
    C) A misinterpretation of dharma texts
    D) Misunderstood Tantric principles

The correct answer is A:) The desire for a certain sex of child. In India, China, Korea and other areas, male children are preferred over female children.

154) What religion did Chuang Tzu's ideas influence?

    A) Confucianism
    B) Taoism
    C) Sikhism
    D) Jainism

The correct answer is B:) Taoism. Chuang Tzu was an influential Chinese philosopher, and his ideas affected Taoist beliefs.

155) Having the right faith, the right conduct, and the right knowledge are known in Jainism as

    A) Dharma
    B) Kharma
    C) Three Jewels
    D) Three Pillars

The correct answer is C:) Three Jewels.

156) When did the Great Schism occur?

    A) 400 AD
    B) 1054 AD
    C) 400 BC
    D) 1054 BC

The correct answer is B:) 1054 AD. This when the church split due to political, cultural, and religious differences.

157) Before the 19th Century, the Slavs spread into Russia. Their thunder-God went by the name

   A) Vila
   B) Rusalki
   C) Perun
   D) Vladamir

The correct answer is C:) Perun.

158) What are the Upanishads?

   A) A group of people with strong devotion to the Rig Veda
   B) The scriptures of the Hindu religion
   C) The philosophical texts of Buddhism
   D) All of the above

The correct answer is B:) The scriptures of the Hindu religion. The Upanishads are indispensable in studying religions of India.

159) Zoroastrism is a religion primarily concerned with

   A) The evil in our hearts
   B) Our Salvation through many deeds
   C) Redemption through one God
   D) The good of God, man, and creation

The correct answer is D:) The good of God, man, and creation.

160) The Sikh community uses this term in reference to itself

   A) Sakhi
   B) Kashrut
   C) Granth
   D) Sila

The correct answer is A:) Sakhi.

　　　© 2012 Breely Crush Publishing, LLC

161) This person is known as the founder of the Christian Science religion.

    A) Dr. Daniel Peterson
    B) Mary Baker Eddy
    C) Ralph Waldo Emerson
    D) None of the above

The correct answer is B:) Mary Baker Eddy.

162) Who was the founder of Zionism?

    A) Abraham Geiger
    B) Milton Steinberg
    C) Theodor Herzl
    D) None of the above

The correct answer is C:) Theodor Herzl. Herzl's book is what strengthened support for Zionism.

163) Hindus believe that much spiritual suffering is caused by a spiritual ignorance known as

    A) Avidya
    B) Samsara
    C) Manidr
    D) Bhakti

The correct answer is A:) Avidya.

164) The ultimate goal of the Baha'i is

    A) Salvation through faith
    B) Unification of mankind
    C) Prepare for the Second Coming
    D) Achieve Enlightenment

The correct answer is B:) Unification of mankind.

165) What is the basic idea of Kabbala?

    A) There are no deeper meanings within the scriptures.
    B) Scriptures can be interpreted in different ways using arrangements of words and numbers to find deeper meanings.
    C) The scriptures were never intended to be interpreted literally.
    D) None of the above

The correct answer is B:) Scriptures can be interpreted in different ways using arrangements of words and numbers to find deeper meanings.

166) Ecclesiastical Law is also known by the Roman Catholic church as

    A) Synodic
    B) Messianic
    C) Catechismic
    D) Canon

The correct answer is D:) Canon.

167) This is the term for the Sikh sect that focuses on asceticism

    A) Udasis
    B) Singhs
    C) Nirankari
    D) Sunni

The correct answer is C:) Nirankari

168) Joseph Smith sat behind a veil, translating aloud the scriptures written on _____, so that they could be transcribed into the Book of Mormon.

    A) Gold Tablets
    B) Seer Stones
    C) The Wall
    D) A Glass Orb

The correct answer is A:) Gold Tablets.

© 2012 Breely Crush Publishing, LLC

169) Who was also known as Father of Many Nations?

    A) Abraham
    B) Isaac
    C) Jacob
    D) All of the above

The correct answer is A:) Abraham. He was told this was what he would be called, along with the promise that he would have a permanent home in the Land of Canaan.

170) Muslims believe in angels. There is the good angel, Gabriel, and a fallen angel known as Shaitan. Shaitan's followers are known as

    A) Jinn
    B) Shi'a
    C) Sanskrit
    D) Vila

The correct answer is A:) Jinn.

171) Even if Roman Catholics do the deeds required of them to go to Heaven, they may end up in _____ to be cleansed of unrepented sin.

    A) Heaven
    B) Hell
    C) Purgatory
    D) Earth

The correct answer is C:) Purgatory.

172) What is the name of God used in the Hebrew Torah?

    A) Yahweh
    B) God
    C) Jehovah
    D) Elohim

The correct answer is D:) Elohim.

173) In Hinduism, what is the name for the 64 deities that attend to Shiva, presiding over enlightenment?

    A) Dharmas
    B) Abhasvaras
    C) Sangitas
    D) Buddhas

The correct answer is B:) Abhasvaras.

174) Most primal religions focus on the question of

    A) Good versus evil
    B) Truth
    C) Enlightenment
    D) Power over life and death

The correct answer is D:) Power over life and death.

175) Why is the word Adonai said in place of Yahweh?

    A) Because Adonai is believed to be a more correct translation.
    B) Because Adonai is easier to say, and means the same thing.
    C) Because Yahweh is believed to be too sacred to pronounce.
    D) None of the above

The correct answer is C:) Because Yahweh is believed to be too sacred to pronounce.

© 2012 Breely Crush Publishing, LLC

🎓 *Test-Taking Strategies*

Here are some test-taking strategies that are specific to this test and to other CLEP tests in general:

- Keep your eyes on the time. Pay attention to how much time you have left.
- Read the entire question and read all the answers. Many questions are not as hard to answer as they may seem. Sometimes, a difficult sounding question really only is asking you how to read an accompanying chart. Chart and graph questions are on most CLEP test and should be an easy free point.
- If you don't know the answer immediately, the new computer-based testing lets you mark questions and come back to them later if you have time.
- Read the wording carefully. Some words can give you hints to the right answer. There are no exceptions to an answer when there are words in the question such as "always" "all" or "none". If one of the answer choices includes most or some of the right answers, but not all, then that is not the answer. Here is an example:

>   The primary colors include all of the following:
>   A) Red, Yellow, Blue, Green
>   B) Red, Green, Yellow
>   C) Red, Orange, Yellow
>   D) Red, Yellow, Blue
>   E) None of the above

   Although item A includes all the right answers, it also includes an incorrect answer, making it incorrect. If you didn't read it carefully, was in a hurry, or didn't know the material well, you might fall for this.
- Make a guess on a question that you do not know the answer to. There is no penalty for an incorrect answer. Eliminate the answer choices that you know are incorrect. For example, this will let your guess be a 1 in 3 chance instead.

🎓 *Test Preparation*

How much you need to study depends on your knowledge of a subject area. If you are interested in literature, took it in school, or enjoy reading then your studying and preparation for the literature or humanities test will not need to be as intensive as someone who is new to literature.

This book is much different than the regular CLEP study guides. This book actually teaches you the information that you need to know to pass the test. If you are particularly interested in an area, or feel like you want more information, do a quick search online. There is a lot you'll need to memorize. Almost everything in this book will be on the test. It is important to understand all major theories and concepts listed in the table of contents. It is also very important to know any bolded words.

Don't worry if you do not understand or know a lot about the area. If you study hard, you can complete and pass the test.

To prepare for the test, make a series of goals. Allot a certain amount of time to review the information you have already studied and to learn additional material. Take notes as you study-it will help you learn the material.

Legal Note

All rights reserved. This Study Guide, Book and Flashcards are protected under US Copyright Law. No part of this book or study guide or flashcards may be reproduced, distributed or stored in a retrieval system, or transmitted in any form or by any means, electronic, mechanical, photocopying, recording, or otherwise, without the prior written permission of the publisher Breely Crush Publishing, LLC. This manual is not supported by or affiliated with the College Board, creators of the CLEP test. CLEP is a registered trademark of the College Entrance Examination Board, which does not endorse this book.

FLASHCARDS

This section contains flashcards for you to use to further your understanding of the material and test yourself on important concepts, names or dates. You can cut these out to study from or keep them in the study guide, flipping the page over to check yourself.